COURSE 3

Chapter 3 Support File

ISBN 0-13-435966-6

Printed in the United States of America.
    5 6 7 8   03 02 01 00

Editorial Services: Visual Education Corporation

Table of Contents

Enrichment/Minds on Math

Backpack Take-Home Activities*

Assessments

Answers to Student Edition Exercises in Overhead-Ready Format

For each lesson, answers are provided for all *On Your Own* and *Mixed Review* Exercises.

Answers to Chapter Support File Pages

*Resource available in Spanish. See *Spanish Resources* booklet.

OBJECTIVES

	Objective	NCTM STANDARDS (see TE p. 114B)	LOCAL STANDARDS
3-1:	To combine like terms; To simplify expressions	1, 2, 3, 4, 9, 12	
3-2:	To solve equations by subtracting; To solve equations by adding	1, 2, 4, 5, 7, 13	
3-3:	To solve equations by dividing; To solve equations by multiplying	1, 2, 4, 5, 9, 13	
3-4:	To solve two-step equations	1, 2, 4, 5, 9, 13	
3-5:	To solve problems by writing an equation	1, 2, 4, 5, 13	
3-6:	To combine like terms and use the distributive property to solve equations	1, 2, 4, 5, 9	
3-7:	To solve equations with variables on both sides of the equal sign	1, 2, 4, 8, 9, 10, 12	
3-8:	To use formulas to solve problems		
	To solve formulas for another variable		
3-9:	To write inequalities; To graph inequalities	1, 2, 3, 4, 5, 13	
	To solve inequalities by subtracting	1, 2, 4, 5, 9, 13	
3-10:	To solve inequalities by adding		
	To solve inequalities by dividing	1, 4, 5, 7, 9, 13	
	To solve inequalities by multiplying		

CHAPTER OVERVIEW

STUDENT EDITION

- Chapter Project, p. 115
- Project Links, pp. 124, 130, 137, 151
- Math Toolboxes, pp. 125, 146
- Problem Solving Practice, p. 152
- Math at Work, p. 130

TEACHER'S EDITION

- Chapter Overview, pp. 114A–114F
  - Pacing Options, p. 114A
  - Chapter Project, Theme, and Goal, p. 114B
  - Meeting Individual Needs, p. 114C
  - Making Connections, p. 114E
    - Interdisciplinary
    - School to Home
  - Technology Options, p. 114E
  - Materials and Manipulatives, p. 114B

TEACHING RESOURCES

- Chapter 3 Support File
  - Lesson Planners
  - Alternative Activities
  - Practice, Reteaching, Enrichment Worksheets
  - Backpack Take-Home Activities*
  - Answers to Student Edition Exercises
  - Multiple-Use Classroom Resources
  - Teaching Aids Masters
  - Tools for Studying Smarter
  - Practice Workbook
  - Transparencies

TECHNOLOGY

- Software
  - *Hot Pages™* 4-3 (use with Lesson 3-3), 4-11 (use with Lesson 3-4), 4-6 (use with Lesson 3-6)
  - Math Investigation: Unidentified Flying Cubes
  - *MathBlaster® Mystery*
  - Interactive Student Tutorial, Chapter 3
  - Resource Pro™, Chapter 3
  - Computer Item Generator, Chapter 3
  - Graphing Calculator Handbook
- Internet
  - The Prentice Hall Math Site is www.phschool.com/math
  - The Web Connection for the Chapter Project is www.phschool.com/mgm3/ch3
- Video
  - Video Field Trips

REVIEW/ASSESSMENT

STUDENT EDITION

- Checkpoints, pp. 134, 156
- Finishing the Chapter Project, p. 161
- Wrap Up, pp. 162–163
- Extra Practice, p. 584
- Chapter Assessment, p. 164
- Cumulative Review, p. 165

TEACHER'S EDITION

- Assessment Options, pp. 114C–114D
  - Standardized Test Correlation, p. 114D
  - Finishing the Chapter Project, p. 161
  - Wrap Up, pp. 162–163
  - Chapter Assessment, pp. 163–164
  - Cumulative Review, p. 165

TEACHING RESOURCES

- Chapter 3 Support File
  - Checkpoints, 1 and 2
  - Student Self-Assessment Survey
  - Performance Assessment and Scoring Rubric
  - Chapter Assessment, Form A*
  - Chapter Assessment, Form B*
  - Cumulative Review

TECHNOLOGY

- Checkpoints, pp. 134, 156
- Finishing the Chapter Project, p. 161
- Wrap Up, pp. 162–163
- Extra Practice, p. 584
- Chapter Assessment, p. 164
- Cumulative Review, p. 165
- Glossary/Study Guide*
- Journal, pp. 124, 134
- Portfolio, p. 160

Lesson Planner 3-1

Simplifying Variable Expressions

1 FOCUS

Warm Up (TE p. 116)

Connecting to Prior Knowledge (TE p. 116)

Students estimate the total amount of money in a bowl. They discuss ways of finding the exact total, looking for the most efficient way.

2 TEACH

Think and Discuss

▼ **Part 1:** *Combining Like Terms* (pp. 116–117)

Example 1 demonstrates how to combine like terms in an algebraic expression.

▼ **Part 2:** *Simplifying Expressions* (pp. 117–118)

Example 2 shows how to simplify an expression. Students see that like terms are combined and as many operations as possible are carried out. Example 3 shows how the distributive property can be used to simplify an expression.

3 PRACTICE/ASSESS

▼ **Part 1**
On Your Own Exercises
  (pp. 118–119)
Core: 1–18
Extension: 19

▼ **Part 2**
On Your Own Exercises
  (pp. 118–119)
Core: 20–38
Extension: 39, 40

• Mixed Review
  (p. 119)
• Lesson Quiz
  (TE p. 119)

OBJECTIVES
• To combine like terms
• To simplify expressions

PREREQUISITE SKILLS
• writing variable expressions (pre-course)
• adding integers (2-3)
• using properties of addition and multiplication (2-8)

MATERIALS/ MANIPULATIVES
• algebra tiles

STANDARDS
• NCTM Standards: Problem Solving, Communication, Reasoning, Mathematical Connections, Algebra, Geometry
• Local Standards: _____
_____

RESOURCE OPTIONS

Teaching Resources	• Chapter 3 Support File	Practice 3-1 Reteaching 3-1 Enrichment/Minds on Math 3-1 Answers to Student Edition Exercises
	• Multiple-Use Classroom Resources	Teaching Aids Masters 26 (Number Lines), 27 (Algebra Tiles)
	• Practice Workbook	Practice 3-1, Enrichment/Minds on Math 3-1
Transparencies	Transparency 8: Number Lines Transparency 51: Enrichment/Minds on Math 3-1	
Technology	Interactive Student Tutorial, Chapter 3 Resource Pro™, 3-1 Computer Item Generator, 3-1 Internet • The Prentice Hall Math Site is www.phschool.com/math.	

Lesson Planner 3-2

Solving Equations by Subtracting or Adding

1 FOCUS

Warm Up (TE p. 120)

Connecting to Prior Knowledge (TE p. 120)

Students relate basic missing addend problems to algebraic equations, substituting a variable for the placeholder that was used in the lower grades.

2 TEACH

Think and Discuss

▼ **Part 1:** *Solving Equations by Subtracting* (pp. 120–121)

Example 1 shows how to solve an equation by subtracting the same quantity from both sides of the equal sign.

▼ **Part 2:** *Solving Equations by Adding* (p. 121)

Example 2 uses a real-world setting to show how to solve an equation by adding the same quantity to each side of the equal sign.

Work Together (p. 122)

Students work in groups to write and solve equations that are described by algebra tiles.

3 PRACTICE/ASSESS

▼ **Part 1**
On Your Own Exercises
 (pp. 122–124)
Core: 1–19
Extension: 20

▼ **Part 2**
On Your Own Exercises
 (pp. 122–124)
Core: 21–45
Extension: 46–58

- Mixed Review
 (p. 124)
- Lesson Quiz
 (TE p. 124)

OBJECTIVES
- To solve equations by subtracting
- To solve equations by adding

PREREQUISITE SKILLS
- adding and subtracting integers (2-3 and 2-4)

MATERIALS/ MANIPULATIVES
- algebra tiles
- calculator

STANDARDS
- NCTM Standards: Problem Solving, Communication, Mathematical Connections, Number and Number Relationships, Computation and Estimation, Measurement
- Local Standards:
 _____
 _____
 _____

Lesson Planner

RESOURCE OPTIONS

Teaching Resources	• Chapter 3 Support File	Practice 3-2 Reteaching 3-2 Enrichment/Minds on Math 3-2 Alternative Activity 3-2 Answers to Student Edition Exercises
	• Multiple-Use Classroom Resources	Teaching Aids Masters 26 (Number Lines), 27 (Algebra Tiles)
	• Practice Workbook	Practice 3-2, Enrichment/Minds on Math 3-2
Transparencies	Transparency 8: Number Lines Transparency 9: Balance Scale Transparency 14: Scientific Calculator Transparency 51: Enrichment/Minds on Math 3-2 Transparency 82: Modeling Equations	
Technology	Graphing Calculator Handbook: Procedure 7 Interactive Student Tutorial, Chapter 3 Resource Pro™, 3-2 Computer Item Generator, 3-2 Internet • The Prentice Hall Math Site is www.phschool.com/math.	

Lesson Planner 3-3

Solving Equations by Dividing or Multiplying

1 FOCUS

Warm Up (TE p. 126)

Connecting to Prior Knowledge (TE p. 126)

Students review the concept of inverse operations. They solve an equation in which the same quantity is added on both sides of the equal sign.

2 TEACH

Work Together (p. 126)

Working in groups, students solve a problem by examining an equation modeled with tiles.

Think and Discuss

▼ **Part 1:** *Solving Equations by Dividing* (pp. 126–127)

Example 1 shows how an equation can be solved by dividing each side of an equation by the same nonzero number. The example reminds students that dividing undoes multiplying.

▼ **Part 2:** *Solving Equations by Multiplying* (p. 128)

Example 2 shows how an equation can be solved by multiplying both sides of an equation by the same number.

3 PRACTICE/ASSESS

▼ **Part 1**
On Your Own Exercises
  (pp. 128–129)
Core: 1–18
Extension: 19, 35

▼ **Part 2**
On Your Own Exercises
  (pp. 128–129)
Core: 20–34, 38–42
Extension: 36, 37, 43

• Mixed Review
  (p. 130)
• Lesson Quiz
  (TE p. 130)

OBJECTIVES
• To solve equations by dividing
• To solve equations by multiplying

PREREQUISITE SKILLS
• multiplying and dividing integers (2-5)
• writing variable expressions (2-2)

MATERIALS/MANIPULATIVES
• algebra tiles

STANDARDS
• NCTM Standards: Problem Solving, Communication, Mathematical Connections, Number and Number Relationships, Algebra, Measurement
• Local Standards:
  _____
  _____
  _____

RESOURCE OPTIONS

Teaching Resources	• Chapter 3 Support File	Practice 3-3 Reteaching 3-3 Enrichment/Minds on Math 3-3 Answers to Student Edition Exercises
	• Multiple-Use Classroom Resources	Teaching Aids Master 27 (Algebra Tiles)
	• Practice Workbook	Practice 3-3, Enrichment/Minds on Math 3-3
Transparencies	Transparency 9: Balance Scale Transparency 14: Scientific Calculator Transparency 51: Enrichment/Minds on Math 3-3 Transparency 82: Modeling Equations	
Technology	Graphing Calculator Handbook: Procedure 7 Hot Page™ 4-3: Multiplication and Division Equations Interactive Student Tutorial, Chapter 3 Resource Pro™, 3-3 Computer Item Generator, 3-3 Internet • The Prentice Hall Math Site is www.phschool.com/math.	

Lesson Planner 3-4

Solving Two-Step Equations

1 Focus

Warm Up (TE p. 131)

Connecting to Prior Knowledge (TE p. 131)

Students consider how a utility company calculates a monthly bill. They discuss the different charges that may be included.

2 Teach

Work Together (p. 131)

Students work in groups to solve a two-step equation using tiles. They represent the inverse operation used at each step.

Think and Discuss

▼ **Part 1:** *Solving Two-Step Equations* (pp. 131–132)

Example 1 shows how to solve a two-step equation by using the inverse operation at each step.

▼ **Part 2:** *Using Two-Step Equations to Solve Problems* (p. 132)

Example 2 shows how a two-step equation can be used to solve a real-world problem. Students see the connection between the word equation and the algebraic equation.

3 Practice/Assess

▼ **Part 1**
On Your Own Exercises
  (pp. 132–134)
Core: 1–24
Extension: 26

▼ **Part 2**
On Your Own Exercises
  (pp. 132–134)
Core: 25, 27–30
Extension: 31

• Mixed Review
  (p. 134)
• Lesson Quiz
  (TE p. 134)
• Checkpoint 1
  (p. 134)

Objectives
• To solve two-step equations
• To use two-step equations to solve problems

Prerequisite Skills
• performing operations with integers (2-3, 2-4, and 2-5)
• solving equations by subtracting, adding, multiplying, or dividing (3-2 and 3-3)

Materials/ Manipulatives
• algebra tiles

Standards
• NCTM Standards: Problem Solving, Communication, Mathematical Connections, Number and Number Relationships, Algebra, Measurement
• Local Standards:
  _____
  _____
  _____

Lesson Planner

Resource Options

Teaching Resources	• Chapter 3 Support File	Practice 3-4 Reteaching 3-4 Enrichment/Minds on Math 3-4 Answers to Student Edition Exercises Checkpoint 1
	• Multiple-Use Classroom Resources	Teaching Aids Master 27 (Algebra Tiles)
	• Practice Workbook	Practice 3-4, Enrichment/Minds on Math 3-4
Transparencies	Transparency 9: Balance Scale Transparency 14: Scientific Calculator Transparency 52: Enrichment/Minds on Math 3-4	
Technology	Graphing Calculator Handbook: Procedure 7 Hot Page™, 4-11: Solving Two-Step Inequalities Interactive Student Tutorial, Chapter 3 Resource Pro™, 3-4 Computer Item Generator, 3-4 Internet • The Prentice Hall Math Site is www.phschool.com/math.	

Lesson Planner 3-5

Problem Solving Strategy: Write an Equation

1 FOCUS

Warm Up (TE p. 135)

Connecting to Prior Knowledge (TE p. 135)

Students discuss strategies they could use to accumulate a given amount of money within a given length of time.

2 TEACH

Think and Discuss (pp. 135–136)

The Sample Problem shows how some problems can be solved by writing an equation. Students see how relationships described in words can be written algebraically.

3 PRACTICE/ASSESS

On Your Own Exercises
(pp. 136–137)
Core: 1–8
Extension: 9, 10

• Mixed Review
(p. 137)
• Lesson Quiz
(TE p. 137)

OBJECTIVE
• To solve problems by writing an equation

PREREQUISITE SKILLS
• writing variable expressions (2-2)
• solving equations (3-2, 3-3, and 3-4)

STANDARDS
• NCTM Standards: Problem Solving, Communication, Mathematical Connections, Number and Number Relationships, Measurement
• Local Standards:
_____
_____
_____

RESOURCE OPTIONS

Teaching Resources ▬	• Chapter 3 Support File Practice 3-5 Reteaching 3-5 Enrichment/Minds on Math 3-5 Answers to Student Edition Exercises • Multiple-Use Classroom Teaching Aids Master 27 (Algebra Tiles) Resources • Practice Workbook Practice 3-5, Enrichment/Minds on Math 3-5
Transparencies	Transparency 52: Enrichment/Minds on Math 3-5 Transparency 83: Writing Equations
Technology	Interactive Student Tutorial, Chapter 3 Resource Pro™, 3-5 Computer Item Generator, 3-5 Internet • The Prentice Hall Math Site is www.phschool.com/math.

Lesson Planner 3-6

Simplifying and Solving Equations

1 FOCUS

Warm Up (TE p. 138)

Connecting to Prior Knowledge (TE p. 138)

Students review simplifying expressions using the distributive property.

2 TEACH

Work Together (p. 138)

Students use algebra tiles to model equations. They use the tiles to simplify the equations by combining like terms.

Think and Discuss

▼ **Part 1:** *Simplifying Before Solving an Equation* (pp. 138–139)

Example 1 shows how to isolate a variable on one side of an equal sign by using properties of equality and inverse operations. Students see how to check the solution to an equation. Example 2 uses a real-world setting to demonstrate how to change word phrases into an equation.

▼ **Part 2:** *Equations with Variables on Both Sides* (pp. 139–140)

Example 3 shows how to solve an equation with a variable on both sides of the equal sign. Students see how to use properties of equality to remove the variable from one side of the equation.

3 PRACTICE/ASSESS

▼ **Part 1**
On Your Own Exercises (pp. 140–141)
Core: 1–17
Extension: 18

▼ **Part 2**
On Your Own Exercises (pp. 140–141)
Core: 21–32
Extension: 19, 20, 33, 34

• Mixed Review (p. 141)
• Lesson Quiz (TE p. 141)

OBJECTIVES
- To combine like terms and use the distributive property to solve equations
- To solve equations with variables on both sides of the equal sign

PREREQUISITE SKILLS
- simplifying expressions (3-1)
- solving two-step equations (3-4)
- performing operations with integers (2-3, 2-4, 2-5)

MATERIALS/ MANIPULATIVES
- algebra tiles

STANDARDS
- NCTM Standards: Problem Solving, Communication, Mathematical Connections, Number and Number Relationships, Algebra
- Local Standards:
  _____
  _____
  _____

Lesson Planner

RESOURCE OPTIONS

Teaching Resources	• Chapter 3 Support File	Practice 3-6 Reteaching 3-6 Enrichment/Minds on Math 3-6 Answers to Student Edition Exercises
	• Multiple-Use Classroom Resources	Teaching Aids Master 27 (Algebra Tiles)
	• Practice Workbook	Practice 3-6, Enrichment/Minds on Math 3-6
Transparencies	Transparency 9: Balance Scale Transparency 14: Scientific Calculator Transparency 52: Enrichment/Minds on Math 3-6	
Technology	Graphing Calculator Handbook: Procedure 7 Hot Page™ 4-6: Simplifying and Solving Equations Interactive Student Tutorial, Chapter 3 Resource Pro™, 3-6 Computer Item Generator, 3-6 Internet • The Prentice Hall Math Site is www.phschool.com/math.	

Lesson Planner 3-7

Formulas

1 FOCUS

Warm Up (TE p. 142)

Connecting to Prior Knowledge (TE p. 142)

Students discuss formulas they have seen or used outside of school.

2 TEACH

Think and Discuss

▼ **Part 1:** *Using Formulas to Solve Problems* (pp. 142–143)

Example 1 shows how to use a formula to find the area of a trapezoid. The example shows that values must be substituted for variables in order to evaluate the formula. In Example 2, students see that it may be necessary to use properties of equality to evaluate a formula.

▼ **Part 2:** *Transforming Formulas* (p. 143)

Example 3 shows how to use properties of equality to transform a formula.

3 PRACTICE/ASSESS

▼ **Part 1**
On Your Own Exercises
 (pp. 144–145)
Core: 1–12
Extension: 14

▼ **Part 2**
On Your Own Exercises
 (pp. 144–145)
Core: 13, 15–25
Extension: 26

• Mixed Review
 (p. 145)
• Lesson Quiz
 (TE p. 145)

OBJECTIVES
• To use formulas to solve problems
• To solve formulas for another variable

PREREQUISITE SKILLS
• performing the order of operations (2-7)
• solving multi-step equations (3-4)

STANDARDS
• NCTM Standards: Problem Solving, Communication, Mathematical Connections, Patterns and Functions, Algebra, Statistics, Geometry
• Local Standards:
_____
_____
_____

RESOURCE OPTIONS

Teaching Resources	• Chapter 3 Support File Practice 3-7 Reteaching 3-7 Enrichment/Minds on Math 3-7 Answers to Student Edition Exercises
	• Practice Workbook Practice 3-7, Enrichment/Minds on Math 3-7
Transparencies	Transparency 14: Scientific Calculator Transparency 53: Enrichment/Minds on Math 3-7
Technology	Graphing Calculator Handbook: Procedure 2 Interactive Student Tutorial, Chapter 3 Resource Pro™, 3-7 Computer Item Generator, 3-7 Internet • The Prentice Hall Math Site is www.phschool.com/math.

Lesson Planner 3-8

Inequalities

Lesson Planner

1 FOCUS

Warm Up (TE p. 147)

Connecting to Prior Knowledge (TE p. 147)

Students recall expressions that they have heard that indicate inequalities, such as *less than*, or *at least*. They name other expressions that express inequalities.

2 TEACH

Work Together (p. 147)

Students work in groups to write inequalities that represent real-world signs.

Think and Discuss

▼ **Part 1:** *Writing Inequalities* (pp. 147–148)

Example 1 shows how to define a variable and write an inequality for a situation. Students see the word relationship transformed into an inequality. The example also shows how to check an inequality.

▼ **Part 2:** *Graphing Inequalities* (pp. 148–149)

Example 2 demonstrates how to graph an inequality on a number line.

> **OBJECTIVES**
> - To write inequalities
> - To graph inequalities
>
> **PREREQUISITE SKILLS**
> - writing equations (3-5)
> - graphing on number lines (pre-course)
>
> **STANDARDS**
> - NCTM Standards: Problem Solving, Communication, Reasoning, Mathematical Connections, Number and Number Relationships, Algebra, Measurement
> - Local Standards: _____ _____ _____

3 PRACTICE/ASSESS

▼ **Part 1**
On Your Own Exercises (pp. 149–151)
Core: 1–18
Extension: 40, 41, 43

▼ **Part 2**
On Your Own Exercises (pp. 149–151)
Core: 19–34, 38, 39, 42
Extension: 35–37

- Mixed Review (p. 151)
- Lesson Quiz (TE p. 151)

RESOURCE OPTIONS

Teaching Resources	• Chapter 3 Support File	Practice 3-8 Reteaching 3-8 Enrichment/Minds on Math 3-8 Answers to Student Edition Exercises
	• Multiple-Use Classroom Resources	Teaching Aids Master 26 (Number Lines)
	• Practice Workbook	Practice 3-8, Enrichment/Minds on Math 3-8
Transparencies	Transparency 8: Number Lines Transparency 53: Enrichment/Minds on Math 3-8	
Technology	Interactive Student Tutorial, Chapter 3 Resource Pro™, 3-8 Computer Item Generator, 3-8 Internet • The Prentice Hall Math Site is www.phschool.com/math.	

Lesson Planner 3-9

Solving Inequalities by Subtracting or Adding

1 FOCUS

Warm Up (TE p. 153)

Connecting to Prior Knowledge (TE p. 153)

Students review solving equations through the use of inverse operations.

2 TEACH

Think and Discuss

▼ **Part 1:** *Solving Inequalities by Subtracting* (pp. 153–154)

Example 1 shows how to use the subtraction property of inequality to solve and graph an inequality.

▼ **Part 2:** *Solving Inequalities by Adding* (p. 154)

In Example 2, the addition property of inequality is used to solve a real-world problem.

3 PRACTICE/ASSESS

▼ **Part 1**
On Your Own Exercises
(pp. 155–156)
Core: 1–4, 6–17
Extension: 18, 19

▼ **Part 2**
On Your Own Exercises
(pp. 155–156)
Core: 5, 20–31
Extension: 32

• Mixed Review
(p. 156)
• Lesson Quiz
(TE p. 156)
• Checkpoint 2
(p. 156)

OBJECTIVES
• To solve inequalities by subtracting
• To solve inequalities by adding

PREREQUISITE SKILLS
• solving equations by adding or subtracting (3-2)
• graphing inequalities (3-8)

STANDARDS
• NCTM Standards: Problem Solving, Communication, Mathematical Connections, Number and Number Relationships, Algebra, Measurement
• Local Standards: _____
_____
_____

RESOURCE OPTIONS

Teaching Resources	• Chapter 3 Support File	Practice 3-9 Reteaching 3-9 Enrichment/Minds on Math 3-9 Answers to Student Edition Exercises Checkpoint 2
	• Multiple-Use Classroom Resources	Teaching Aids Master 26 (Number Lines)
	• Practice Workbook	Practice 3-9, Enrichment/Minds on Math 3-9
Transparencies	Transparency 8: Number Lines Transparency 14: Scientific Calculator Transparency 53: Enrichment/Minds on Math 3-9	
Technology	Interactive Student Tutorial, Chapter 3 Resource Pro™, 3-9 Computer Item Generator, 3-9 Internet • The Prentice Hall Math Site is www.phschool.com/math.	

Lesson Planner 3-10

Solving Inequalities by Dividing or Multiplying

1 FOCUS

Warm Up (TE p. 157)

Connecting to Prior Knowledge (TE p. 157)

Students discuss using inverse operations to solve multiplication and division equations.

2 TEACH

Work Together (p. 157)

Students look for patterns in the use of inequality signs. They explore the effect on an inequality of multiplying or dividing each side by a positive number. They compare findings to what happens when both sides are multiplied or divided by a negative number.

Think and Discuss

▼ **Part 1:** *Solving Inequalities by Dividing* (pp. 157–158)

Example 1 shows the use of the division properties for inequalities. Students see that when both sides of an inequality are divided by a negative number, the direction of the inequality reverses. Example 2 shows how to apply the division properties of inequalities to a real-world problem.

▼ **Part 2:** *Solving Inequalities by Multiplying* (p. 159)

Example 3 shows the use of the multiplication properties for inequalities. Students see that when both sides are multiplied by a negative number, the direction of the inequality reverses.

3 PRACTICE/ASSESS

▼ **Part 1**
On Your Own Exercises
 (pp. 159–160)
Core: 1–16
Extension: 36

▼ **Part 2**
On Your Own Exercises
 (pp. 159–160)
Core: 17–31, 37, 39
Extension: 32–35, 38

• Mixed Review
 (p. 160)
• Lesson Quiz
 (TE p. 160)

OBJECTIVES
• To solve inequalities by dividing
• To solve inequalities by multiplying

PREREQUISITE SKILLS
• solving equations by dividing or multiplying (3-3)
• graphing inequalities (3-8)

STANDARDS
• NCTM Standards: Problem Solving, Mathematical Connections, Number and Number Relationships, Computation and Estimation, Algebra, Measurement
• Local Standards:
  _____
  _____
  _____

Lesson Planner

RESOURCE OPTIONS

Teaching Resources	• Chapter 3 Support File	Practice 3-10 Reteaching 3-10 Enrichment/Minds on Math 3-10 Alternative Activity 3-10 Answers to Student Edition Exercises
	• Multiple-Use Classroom Resources	Teaching Aids Master 26 (Number Lines)
	• Practice Workbook	Practice 3-10, Enrichment/Minds on Math 3-10
Transparencies	Transparency 8: Number Lines Transparency 14: Scientific Calculator Transparency 53: Enrichment/Minds on Math 3-10	
Technology	Interactive Student Tutorial, Chapter 3 Resource Pro™, 3-10 Computer Item Generator, 3-10 Internet • The Prentice Hall Math Site is www.phschool.com/math.	

Technology Activity 3-2 *Teacher's Notes*

Addition and Subtraction Equations

What's Ahead: Solving one-step equations using addition and subtraction

Materials: computer, spreadsheet software, Transparency 3 (Spreadsheet Database Form), teacher-made transparency of Student Worksheet

Teacher Does	Teacher Says	Student Responses
Place Transparency 3 on the overhead. Write: $m + 2 = 6$	An **equation** is a mathematical sentence with an equal sign. In an equation like $m + 2 = 6$, a value of the variable that makes the equation true is called a **solution** of the equation. We can solve $m + 2 = 6$ using an algebra tile model.	
Draw the following model on the transparency.	What is the result if you remove two squares from each side of the equation? What is the solution of the equation?	an m-tile on the left and four square tiles on the right 4
Write the following solution on the transparency under the equation. $m + 2 - 2 = 6 - 2$ $m = 4$	To solve equations using algebra, you use the fact that addition and subtraction are inverse operations. You can use subtraction to "undo" an addition, and the result is an *equivalent equation*. The Subtraction Property of Equality states that if you subtract the same number from each side of an equation, the results are equal.	

Teacher Does	Teacher Says	Student Responses
Label column A "Solution" and column B "Check."	We can also use a computer and a spreadsheet to solve an equation. What will you enter into cell A2 to solve this equation? What will you enter into cell B2 to check this solution? How will you use the check to be sure the solution is correct?	$=6-2$ $=A2+2$ The solution is correct if the number in cell B2 is 6.

	A	B	C
1	Solution	Check	
2			
3			
4			
5			
6			
7			

Teacher Does	Teacher Says	Student Responses
Enter the values on the transparency.		

	A	B	C
1	Solution	Check	
2	4	6	
3			
4			
5			
6			
7			

Have students duplicate the spreadsheet on a computer.

Activity (individuals or small groups)

Teacher Does	Teacher Says	Student Responses
Use a clean copy of Transparency 3. Use the same labels. Write the following equation on the bottom half of the transparency. $x - 5 = -4$	Addition can be used to "undo" a subtraction. The Addition Property of Equality states that if you add the same number to each side of an equation, the results are equal. Decide how you could use the spreadsheet to help you solve the equation and check the solution. Complete the worksheet.	

Summarize

Teacher Does	Teacher Says	Student Responses
	What did you do to solve the equation?	Added 5 to both sides of the equation.

Alternative Activity

Teacher Does	Teacher Says	Student Responses
Have a student show how to solve and check the equation. Write the solution and check on the transparency. $x - 5 + 5 = -4 + 5$ $x = 1$ Check: $x - 5 = -4$ $1 - 5 = -4$ $-4 = -4$	How can you use the spreadsheet to help you solve the equation? How can you use the spreadsheet to help you check the solution?	Enter =−4+5 into cell A2. Enter =A2−5 into cell B2. If the solution in cell A2 is correct, the number in cell B2 should be −4.

	A	B	C
1	Solution	Check	
2	1	−4	
3			
4			
5			
6			
7			

Have students duplicate the spreadsheet on a computer.

Use your computer spreadsheet to do Exercises 1-4. Print out your spreadsheet, or enter your data in the spreadsheet on your worksheet. Then do Exercises 5-9.

Solve the Problem

Teacher Does	Teacher Says	Student Responses
Have students come together. Place the transparency of the Student Worksheet on the overhead. Ask a student to read the problem. Review completed spreadsheets with students.	What have we learned that will help us find the answer to this problem? How can you use a spreadsheet to do this?	Read the problem carefully and write an equation. Solve the equation by doing the same thing to both sides to "undo" the operation. Use a spreadsheet to solve the equation and check the solution.

Technology Activity 3-2 Student Worksheet

Addition and Subtraction Equations

	A	B	C
1			
2			
3			
4			
5			
6			
7			

Exercises

Solve each equation. Use a spreadsheet to check.

1. $-18 + m = 76$ _____   **2.** $t + 35 = -22$ _____

3. $-3.94 = y - 5.77$ _____   **4.** $w + \frac{3}{4} = \frac{1}{2}$ _____

Choose from -30, -20, -10, 0, 10, 20, and 30. Find all the numbers that are solutions of each equation. Use a spreadsheet to check your answers.

5. $|y| = 20$ _____   **6.** $|y| + 10 = 20$ _____

7. $|d + 20| = 10$ _____

Write an equation for each problem. Solve the equation. Then give the solution of the problem.

8. Yesterday Kevin delivered some neighborhood newsletters. Today he delivered 15 more newsletters. If Kevin delivered 38 newsletters in all, how many did he deliver yesterday?

_____

9. After Georgia spent $5.65 on lunch, she had $9.35 left. How much money did she have to begin with?

_____

The Problem

Ben put a deposit of $6.75 on a coat he put in layaway. He now owes $56.50 on the coat. Write and solve an equation to find the total cost of the coat. _____

Math Connection Activity 3-10 *Teacher's Notes*

Science: Solving Inequalities

What's Ahead: Solving one-step inequalities and graphing the solutions on a number line

Writing one-step inequalities with one variable

Materials: teacher-made transparency of Student Worksheet

Teacher Does	Teacher Says	Student Responses
Concentrate the discussion on the work of geologists.	A geologist studies all aspects of Earth, including soil and rocks and their composition. Can you think of why a geologist's work is necessary?	Answers may vary. Possible answers: when drilling for oil or water, when testing the soil to see if it will hold a building or tower
Introduce a problem to explain the addition and subtraction properties for inequalities.	Let's suppose that we have drilled in the ground one hole 12 ft deep and another 16 ft deep. But we have to drill both holes 5 ft deeper. Which hole will now be deeper?	the hole that was 16 ft at the beginning
Write an inequality to explain the example.	We can write this problem: 12 < 16 12 + 5 < 16 + 5 17 < 21 Has the inequality changed?	If we add a number to each side of an inequality, the inequality remains true.
Extend the example to look at the subtraction property for inequalities.	If we next had to bring the drills back up 11 ft, which drill would then be deeper in the ground?	the drill that was deeper in the ground to begin with
Write an inequality to explain the example.	We can write this example : 17 < 21 17 − 11 < 21 − 11 6 < 10 What happened?	If we subtract a number from both sides of an inequality, the inequality remains true.
Write and explain the algebraic representation for the addition and subtraction properties for inequalities.	We can go one step further and write these inequalities algebraically.	

Teacher Does	Teacher Says	Student Responses
If $a > b$, then $a + c > b + c$ If $a < b$, then $a + c < b + c$ If $a > b$, then $a - c > b - c$ If $a < b$, then $a - c < b - c$	For addition, we can write the **Addition Properties for Inequalities.** We can also write the **Subtraction Properties for Inequalities.**	

Activity (individual or small groups)

Teacher Does	Teacher Says	Student Responses
Look at an example where the subtraction property for inequalities can be used. Write: $\quad x + 19 \geq 30$ $x + 19 - 19 \geq 30 - 19$ $\quad\quad x \geq 11$	Now let's use these properties. First, if you want to drill a hole at least 30 ft deep and have already drilled 19 ft, write and solve an inequality to represent how much farther you need to drill. Use the subtraction property for inequalities. How much farther do we need to drill? Graph this solution on your worksheet.	We need to drill 11 more feet.
Explain the multiplication and division properties for inequalities.	Suppose that in two soil samples taken, 30% of the composition was sand. The first sample weighed 18 g and the second sample weighed 21 g. Does the soil sample that weighs more also have a greater amount of sand by weight? Explain your answer.	Yes, because the percentage of sand is the same in each sample.
Look at the problem numerically. Write: $\quad 18 < 21$ $18(0.3) < 21(0.3)$ $\quad 5.4 < 6.3$ Extend this problem to look at the division property for inequalities.	We can represent the situation with an inequality. So the sample that was heavier originally does have more sand by weight. If we only used $\frac{1}{4}$ the amount of each of the original soil samples, does the second sample of sand still weigh more? Explain.	Yes, because the percentage of sand is the same in each sample.

Alternative Activity

Teacher Does	Teacher Says	Student Responses
Write: $18 < 21$ $\frac{18}{4} < \frac{21}{4}$ $4.5 < 5.25$	We can write the problem numerically.	
	Do you think the inequality will remain true if we multiply or divide an inequality by a negative number?	Answers may vary.
Write: $8 > 4$ $8(-2) > 4\,(-2)$ $-16 > -8$ $-12 < -9$ $\frac{-12}{-3} < \frac{-9}{-3}$ $4 < 3$	Let's look at some examples. Then we can decide if they are true or false. This is false. This is also false.	

Summarize

Write: Multiplication Properties are: If $a > b$ and $c > 0$, then $ac > bc$. If $a < b$ and $c > 0$, then $ac < bc$. If $a > b$ and $c < 0$, then $ac < bc$. If $a < b$ and $c < 0$, then $ac > bc$. The Division Properties are: If $a > b$ and $c > 0$, then $\frac{a}{c} > \frac{b}{c}$. If $a < b$ and $c > 0$, then $\frac{a}{c} < \frac{b}{c}$. If $a > b$ and $c < 0$, then $\frac{a}{c} < \frac{b}{c}$. If $a < b$ and $c < 0$, then $\frac{a}{c} > \frac{b}{c}$.	From these examples, we can write the **Multiplication Properties for Inequalities** and the **Division Properties for Inequalities.**	

Solve the Problem

Have a student read the problem.	Use what you have learned in this lesson to solve the problem.	

Math Connection Activity 3-10 Student Worksheet

Science: Solving Inequalities

Exercises

1. Graph the solutions for the first example in the lesson. Then graph the other solutions.

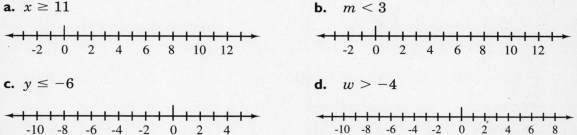

a. $x \geq 11$

b. $m < 3$

c. $y \leq -6$

d. $w > -4$

The Problem

During an exploration, you and your group of geologists collected an assortment of rocks to check their composition. You did not know, however, that you only needed at least 4 lb of samples for testing. As a result, you realize that $\frac{1}{6}$ of the amount of rocks that you have collected is more than enough. Write an inequality to find at least how many pounds of rocks you have collected. Then solve the inequality and graph it.

_____

_____

```
<-+--+--+--+--+--+--+--+--+--+--+--+--+->
   -4   0   4   8   12  16  20  24
```

Suppose that in an ordinary expedition, you need to collect more than four times the weight in rock samples that are needed for testing because some will not be acceptable. For this expedition, you need to collect more than 12 lb of rock samples to ensure that you have collected enough for testing. Write an inequality to find at least how many pounds of rocks will be acceptable. Then solve the inequality and graph it.

_____

_____

```
<-+--+--+--+--+--+--+--+--+--+--+--+--+->
  -2   0   2   4   6   8   10  12
```

▄▄▄▄▄▄ *Practice 3-1* Simplifying Variable Expressions

Simplify each expression.

1. $4a + 7 + 2a$

_____

2. $8(k - 9)$

_____

3. $5n + 6n - 2n$

_____

4. $(w + 3)7$

_____

5. $5(b - 6) + 9$

_____

6. $-4 + 8(2 + t)$

_____

7. $-4 + 3(6 + k)$

_____

8. $12j - 9j$

_____

9. $6(d - 8)$

_____

10. $-9 + 8(x + 6)$

_____

11. $4(m + 6) - 3$

_____

12. $27 + 2(f - 19)$

_____

13. $4v - 7 + 8v + 4 - 5$

_____

14. $5(g + 8) + 7 + 4g$

_____

15. $12h - 17 - h + 16 - 2h$

_____

16. $7(e - 8) + 12 - 2e$

_____

17. $-3y + 7 + y + 6y$

_____

18. $(3.2m + 1.8) - 1.07m$

_____

Choose a calculator, paper and pencil, or mental math to simplify each expression.

19. $28k + 36(7 + k)$

_____

20. $3.09(j + 4.6)$

_____

21. $12b + 24(b - 42)$

_____

22. $7.9y + 8.4 - 2.04y$

_____

23. $4.3(5.6 + c)$

_____

24. $83x + 15(x - 17)$

_____

25. $9.8c + 8d - 4.6c + 2.9d$

_____

26. $18 + 27m - 29 + 36m$

_____

27. $8(j + 12) + 4(k - 19)$

_____

28. $4.2r + 8.1s + 1.09r + 6.32s$

_____

29. $43 + 16c - 18d + 56c + 16d$

_____

30. $9(a + 14) + 8(b - 16)$

_____

31. Tyrone bought 15.3 gal of gasoline priced at g dollars per gal, 2 qt of oil priced at q dollars per qt, and a wiper blade priced at $3.79. Write an expression that represents the total cost of these items.

_____

32. Choose a number. Multiply by 2. Add 6 to the product. Divide by 2. Then subtract 3. What is the answer? Repeat this process using two different numbers. Explain what happened.

_____

_____

_____

Practice 3-2 Solving Equations by Subtracting or Adding

Choose a calculator, paper and pencil, or mental math to solve each equation. Check the solution.

1. $x - 6 = -18$

2. $-14 = 8 + j$

3. $4.19 + w = 19.72$

4. $b + \frac{1}{6} = \frac{7}{8}$

5. $9 + k = 27$

6. $14 + t = -17$

7. $v - 2.59 = 26$

8. $r + 9 = 15$

9. $n - 19 = 26$

10. $14 = -3 + s$

11. $9 = d - 4.3$

12. $g - \frac{1}{4} = \frac{5}{8}$

13. $15 + y = -4$

14. $8.17 + d = 14.2$

15. $f - 19 = 14$

16. $-19 = a - 14$

17. $-2 = g + 21$

18. $h - 9.2 = 7.3$

19. $c - 9.02 = -8.6$

20. $b + 31 = -8$

21. $14 = i - 27$

22. $-41 = n - 18$

23. $p + \frac{3}{4} = \frac{9}{10}$

24. $-4 = w + 16$

Write an equation for each problem. Solve the equation. Then give the solution of the problem.

25. Yesterday Josh sold some boxes of greeting cards. Today he sold seven boxes. If he sold 25 boxes in all, how many did he sell yesterday?

26. After Hoshi spent $27.98 for a sweater, she had $18.76 left. How much money did she have to begin with?

27. After Simon donated four books to the school library, he had 28 books left. How many books did Simon have to start with?

28. One day Reeva baked several dozen muffins. The next day she made 8 dozen more muffins. If she made 20 dozen muffins in all, how many dozen did she make the first day?

Practice

Practice 3-3 *Solving Equations by Dividing or Multiplying*

Choose a calculator, paper and pencil, or mental math to solve each equation. Check the solution.

1. $\dfrac{a}{-6} = 2$ _____

2. $18 = \dfrac{v}{-1.8}$ _____

3. $46 = 2.3m$ _____

4. $-114 = -6k$ _____

5. $0 = \dfrac{b}{19}$ _____

6. $136 = 8y$ _____

7. $0.6j = -1.44$ _____

8. $\dfrac{q}{7.4} = 8.3$ _____

9. $28b = -131.6$ _____

10. $\dfrac{n}{-9} = -107$ _____

11. $37c = -777$ _____

12. $\dfrac{n}{-1.28} = 4.96$ _____

13. $53k = -3,816$ _____

14. $\dfrac{e}{-8.6} = -9.04$ _____

15. $-12j = 90$ _____

16. $\dfrac{q}{7.4} = -8.9$ _____

17. $5.7b = 11.742$ _____

18. $\dfrac{c}{-19} = 25$ _____

19. $43b = -3,397$ _____

20. $\dfrac{s}{-19.6} = 2.04$ _____

21. $-8.05d = 198.03$ _____

22. $\dfrac{f}{87} = 93$ _____

23. $56.4w = 163.56$ _____

24. $\dfrac{g}{-47} = 105$ _____

25. $\dfrac{b}{-7} = 17$ _____

26. $12z = -60$ _____

27. $\dfrac{k}{9.2} = 7.6$ _____

28. $17y = -153$ _____

Write an equation for each problem. Solve the equation. Then give the solution of the problem.

29. Twelve notebooks cost $15.48 in all. What is the price of one notebook?

_____

30. Skylar bought seven books at $12.95 each. How much did Skylar spend?

_____

31. Clarinda has to make 96 treats for school. How many dozen treats is this?

_____

32. Eugenio has five payments left to make on his computer. If each payment is $157.90, how much does he still owe?

_____

Name _____ Class _____ Date _____

Practice 3-4 Solving Two-Step Equations

**Choose a calculator, paper and pencil, or mental math to
solve each equation. Check the solution.**

1. $4r + 6 = 14$

2. $9y - 11 = 7$

3. $\frac{m}{4} + 6 = 3$

4. $\frac{k}{-9} + 6 = -4$

5. $-5b - 6 = -11$

6. $\frac{v}{-7} + 8 = 19$

7. $3.4t + 19.36 = -10.22$

8. $\frac{n}{-1.6} + 7.9 = 8.4$

9. $4.6b + 26.8 = 50.72$

10. $\frac{a}{-8.06} + 7.02 = 18.4$

11. $-2.06d + 18 = -10.84$

12. $\frac{e}{-95} + 6 = 4$

13. $-9i - 17 = -26$

14. $\frac{j}{-1.9} + 2.7 = -8.6$

15. $14.9 = 8.6 + 0.9m$

16. $84 = 19 + \frac{z}{12}$

17. $15w - 21 = -111$

18. $-12.4 = -19.1 + \frac{n}{-7.9}$

19. Hugo received $100 for his birthday. He
then saved $20 per week until he had a
total of $460 to buy a printer. Use an
equation to show how many weeks it
took him to save the money.

_____

20. A health club charges a $50 initial fee
plus $2 for each visit. Moselle has
spent a total of $144 at the health
club this year. Use an equation to
find how many visits she has made.

_____

**Solve each equation to find the value of the variable. Write
the answer in the puzzle. Do not include any negative
signs or any decimal points.**

Across

1. $6n - 12 = 2.4$

2. $\frac{n}{3} + 4.6 = 21.6$

4. $x - 3 = 51.29$

6. $2z + 2 = 7.6$

Down

1. $\frac{j}{5} - 14 = -9$

2. $3x - 2 = 169$

3. $\frac{x}{4} + 1 = 19$

4. $\frac{x}{3} + 4 = 22$

5. $2x - 2 = 182$

Practice

Course 3 Chapter 3

■■■ *Practice 3-5* *Problem-Solving Strategy:*
Write an Equation

Write an equation to solve each problem. Check the solution.

1. The cost of a long-distance phone call is $.56 for the first minute and $.32 for each additional minute. What was the total length of a call that cost $9.20?

   _____

2. A house sits on a rectangular piece of land. Two of the sides measure 104 ft each. If all four sides add to 576 ft, how long is each of the other two sides?

   _____

3. A gas tank contains 12.6 gal of gas. If this is $\frac{4}{5}$ of the gas tank's capacity, how many gallons can the tank hold?

   _____

4. If you subtract 9.4 from a third of a number, the result is 8.7. What is the number?

   _____

Choose any strategy to solve each problem. Show all your work.

5. Mary and Jim have tickets to a concert. Mary's ticket number is one less than Jim's ticket number. The product of their numbers is 812. What are the two numbers?

   _____

6. The Beards' budget is shown at the right. Their house payment is raised $120. Their income will be no more than it is now, so they plan on subtracting an equal amount from each of the other categories. How much will be available to spend on bills?

Beards' Budget	
Item	**Amount**
House	$650
Food	$300
Bills	$250
Other	$140

   _____

7. Antonio watches $\frac{2}{3}$ of a movie at home and then decides to finish watching it later. If he already has watched 2 hours of the movie, how long is it?

   _____

Practice 3-6 Simplifying and Solving Equations

Write an equation that can be modeled by the tiles. Solve the equation.

1.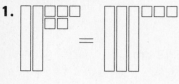

_____

2.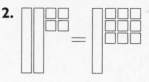

_____

Choose a calculator, paper and pencil, or mental math to solve each equation. Check the solution.

3. $2(2.5b - 9) + 6b = -7$

_____

4. $12y = 2y + 40$

_____

5. $6(c + 4) = 4c - 18$

_____

6. $0.7w + 16 + 4w = 27.28$

_____

7. $24 = -6(m + 1) + 18$

_____

8. $0.5m + 6.4 = 4.9 - 0.1m$

_____

9. $7k - 8 + 2(k + 12) = 52$

_____

10. $14b = 16(b + 12)$

_____

11. $4(1.5c + 6) - 2c = -9$

_____

12. $7y = y - 42$

_____

13. $9(d - 4) = 5d + 8$

_____

14. $0.5n + 17 + n = 20$

_____

15. $20 = -4(f + 6) + 14$

_____

16. $12j = 16(j - 8)$

_____

17. $0.7p + 4.6 = 7.3 - 0.2p$

_____

18. $9a - 4 + 3(a - 11) = 23$

_____

19. $6(f + 5) = 2f - 8$

_____

20. $15p = 6(p - 9)$

_____

21. $0.5t + 4.1 = 5.7 - 0.3t$

_____

22. $9q - 14 + 3(q - 8) = 7$

_____

Practice 3-7 Formulas

Write appropriate formulas to find the perimeter and
area of each figure. Then find the perimeter and area of
each figure.

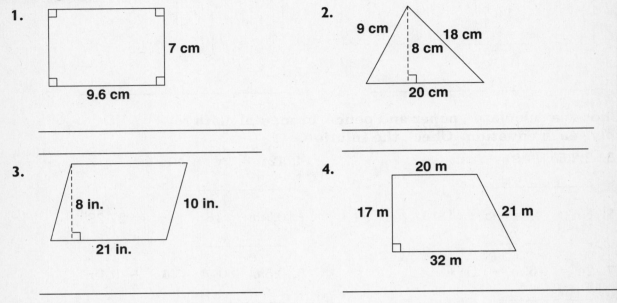

1.

7 cm

9.6 cm

_____

_____

2.

9 cm   18 cm

8 cm

20 cm

_____

_____

3.

8 in.   10 in.

21 in.

_____

_____

4.

20 m

17 m   21 m

32 m

_____

_____

Write an equation to find the the solution for each problem.
Solve the equation. Then give the solution for the problem.

5. The Kents left home at 7:00 A.M. and
drove to their parents' house 400 mi
away. They arrived at 3:00 P.M. What
was their average speed?

_____

6. An airplane flew for 4 h 30 min at an
average speed of 515 mi/h. How far
did it fly?

_____

7. Marcia rowed her boat 18 mi downstream at a rate of
12 mi/h. How long did the trip take?

_____

In Exercises 8–11, use the formula $F = \frac{9}{5}C + 32$ or
$C = \frac{5}{9}(F - 32)$ to find a temperature in either
degrees Fahrenheit, °F, or degrees Celsius, °C.

8. What is the temperature in degrees
Fahrenheit when it is 0°C?

_____

9. What is the temperature in degrees
Fahrenheit when it is 100°C?

_____

10. What is the temperature in degrees
Celsius when it is −4°F?

_____

11. What is the temperature in degrees
Celsius when it is 77°F?

_____

Practice 3-8 Inequalities

Write an inequality for each graph.

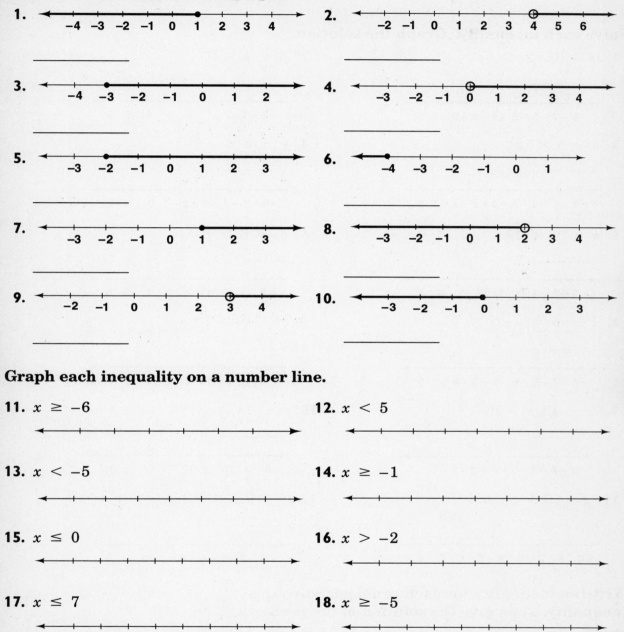

1.

_____

2.

_____

3.

_____

4.

_____

5.

_____

6.

_____

7.

_____

8.

_____

9.

_____

10.

_____

Graph each inequality on a number line.

11. $x \geq -6$

12. $x < 5$

13. $x < -5$

14. $x \geq -1$

15. $x \leq 0$

16. $x > -2$

17. $x \leq 7$

18. $x \geq -5$

Practice

Practice 3-9 Solving Inequalities by Subtracting or Adding

Solve each inequality. Graph the solution.

1. $m + 6 > 2$

_____

$-8\ -7\ -6\ -5\ -4\ -3\ -2\ -1\ 0$

2. $q + 4 \le 9$

_____

$-2\ -1\ 0\ 1\ 2\ 3\ 4\ 5\ 6$

3. $w - 6 > -9$

_____

$-8\ -7\ -6\ -5\ -4\ -3\ -2\ -1\ 0$

4. $y - 3 < -4$

_____

$-6\ -5\ -4\ -3\ -2\ -1\ 0\ 1\ 2$

5. $k + 9 \le 12$

_____

$-3\ -2\ -1\ 0\ 1\ 2\ 3\ 4\ 5$

6. $u + 6 \ge 8$

_____

$-2\ -1\ 0\ 1\ 2\ 3\ 4\ 5\ 6$

7. $x - 9 < -12$

_____

$-8\ -7\ -6\ -5\ -4\ -3\ -2\ -1\ 0$

8. $d + 9 \ge 10$

_____

$-2\ -1\ 0\ 1\ 2\ 3\ 4\ 5\ 6$

9. $h - 12 < -15$

_____

$-8\ -7\ -6\ -5\ -4\ -3\ -2\ -1\ 0$

10. $e + 14 \ge 24$

_____

$8\ 9\ 10\ 11\ 12\ 13\ 14\ 15\ 16$

11. $g - 9.6 \le -4.6$

_____

$0\ 1\ 2\ 3\ 4\ 5\ 6\ 7\ 8$

12. $r + 7.1 > 2.1$

_____

$-8\ -7\ -6\ -5\ -4\ -3\ -2\ -1\ 0$

Write an inequality for each problem. Solve the inequality. Then give the solution of the problem.

13. The amount of snow on the ground increased by 8 in. between 7 P.M. and 10 P.M. By 10 P.M., there was less than 2 ft of snow. How much snow was there by 7 P.M.?

_____

14. The school record for points scored in a basketball season by one player is 462. Maria has 235 points so far this season. How many more points does she need to break the record?

_____

Practice 3-10 Solving Inequalities by Dividing or Multiplying

Solve each inequality. Graph the solution.

1. $-5m < 20$

_____

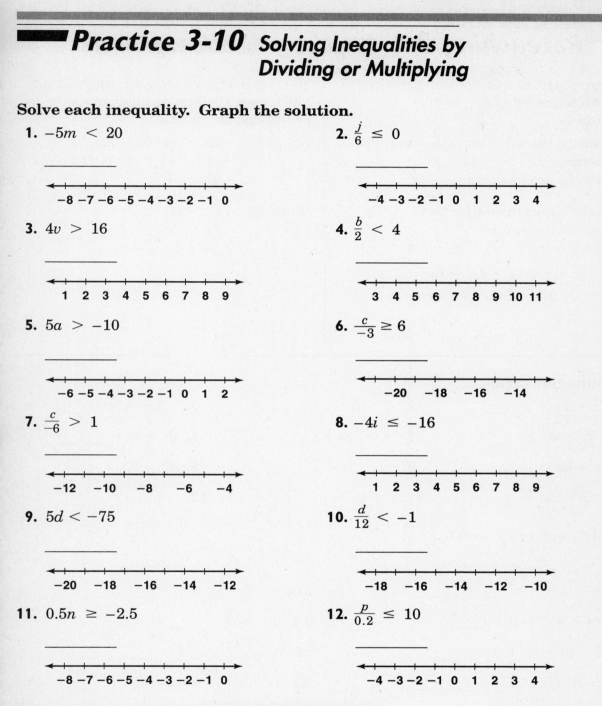

$\begin{array}{ccccccccc} \text{-8} & \text{-7} & \text{-6} & \text{-5} & \text{-4} & \text{-3} & \text{-2} & \text{-1} & \text{0} \end{array}$

2. $\frac{j}{6} \le 0$

_____

$\begin{array}{ccccccccc} \text{-4} & \text{-3} & \text{-2} & \text{-1} & \text{0} & \text{1} & \text{2} & \text{3} & \text{4} \end{array}$

3. $4v > 16$

_____

$\begin{array}{ccccccccc} \text{1} & \text{2} & \text{3} & \text{4} & \text{5} & \text{6} & \text{7} & \text{8} & \text{9} \end{array}$

4. $\frac{b}{2} < 4$

_____

$\begin{array}{ccccccccc} \text{3} & \text{4} & \text{5} & \text{6} & \text{7} & \text{8} & \text{9} & \text{10} & \text{11} \end{array}$

5. $5a > -10$

_____

$\begin{array}{ccccccccc} \text{-6} & \text{-5} & \text{-4} & \text{-3} & \text{-2} & \text{-1} & \text{0} & \text{1} & \text{2} \end{array}$

6. $\frac{c}{-3} \ge 6$

_____

$\begin{array}{cccc} \text{-20} & \text{-18} & \text{-16} & \text{-14} \end{array}$

7. $\frac{c}{-6} > 1$

_____

$\begin{array}{ccccc} \text{-12} & \text{-10} & \text{-8} & \text{-6} & \text{-4} \end{array}$

8. $-4i \le -16$

_____

$\begin{array}{ccccccccc} \text{1} & \text{2} & \text{3} & \text{4} & \text{5} & \text{6} & \text{7} & \text{8} & \text{9} \end{array}$

9. $5d < -75$

_____

$\begin{array}{ccccc} \text{-20} & \text{-18} & \text{-16} & \text{-14} & \text{-12} \end{array}$

10. $\frac{d}{12} < -1$

_____

$\begin{array}{ccccc} \text{-18} & \text{-16} & \text{-14} & \text{-12} & \text{-10} \end{array}$

11. $0.5n \ge -2.5$

_____

$\begin{array}{ccccccccc} \text{-8} & \text{-7} & \text{-6} & \text{-5} & \text{-4} & \text{-3} & \text{-2} & \text{-1} & \text{0} \end{array}$

12. $\frac{p}{0.2} \le 10$

_____

$\begin{array}{ccccccccc} \text{-4} & \text{-3} & \text{-2} & \text{-1} & \text{0} & \text{1} & \text{2} & \text{3} & \text{4} \end{array}$

Write an inequality for each problem. Solve the inequality. Then give the solution of the problem.

13. Dom wants to buy 5 baseballs. He has $20. What is the most each baseball can cost?

_____

14. A typing service charges $5.00 per page. Mrs. Garza does not want to spend more than $50 for the typing. What is the maximum number of pages she can have typed?

_____

Reteaching 3-1 Simplifying Variable Expressions

A **term** is part of a variable expression. The two terms in $-2x + 4y$ are $-2x$ and $4y$.

Terms with the same variable are called **like terms.** In $-3x + 4y + 5x$, $-3x$ and $5x$ are like terms.

One way to **combine like terms** is by addition or subtraction.
• Add to combine like terms in $4y + y$.

$$4y + y = (4 + 1)y = 5y$$

• Subtract to combine like terms in $2m - 5m$.

$$2m - 5m = (2 - 5)m = -3m$$

To **simplify** an expression, combine its like terms. Perform as many of its operations as possible.

Simplify:
$$3a + 5b - a + 2b$$
$$= (3a - a) + (5b + 2b)$$
$$= 2a + 7b$$

Simplify:
$$2(x - 4)$$
$$= 2x - 2(4)$$
$$= 2x - 8$$

Combine like terms.

1. $6x + 2x = $ _____

2. $4c - c = $ _____

3. $-h - h = $ _____

4. $-3y + 4y = $ _____

5. $m - 5m = $ _____

6. $6n + n = $ _____

7. $2s - 6s = $ _____

8. $-t - 2t = $ _____

9. $3b - 9b = $ _____

10. $-2p - 5p = $ _____

11. $v + 9v = $ _____

12. $-4j + j = $ _____

Simplify each expression.

13. $8(c - 5) = $ _____

14. $4(d + 6) = $ _____

15. $5n + 3 + n = $ _____

16. $x + 2y + x + y = $ _____

17. $3m + 4 - 5m = $ _____

18. $(v - 4)5 = $ _____

19. $4a + 2 - 8a + 1 = $ _____

20. $6s + 5 - s - 6 = $ _____

21. $3(u + 4) - 5u = $ _____

22. $2x + y - 9 + 4x = $ _____

23. $-5x + 3(x - y) = $ _____

24. $v + 6v - 2v = $ _____

25. $-2s + 6 - s - 4 = $ _____

26. $-x + 4(x + 2) = $ _____

27. $3k + j - 4k - k = $ _____

28. $4a - 6 - a + 1 = $ _____

▰▰▰Reteaching 3-2 Solving Equations by Subtracting or Adding

To solve equations by subtraction or addition:

① Use opposite, or inverse, operations to isolate the variable.

② Simplify.

③ Check by substituting your answer for the variable.

Solve and check each equation.

$$x + 7 = 34$$
$$x + 7 - 7 = 34 - 7 \leftarrow \textbf{Subtract 7 from each side.}$$
$$x = 27 \qquad \leftarrow \textbf{Simplify.}$$

Check: $\quad x + 7 = 34$
$$27 + 7 \overset{?}{=} 34$$
$$34 = 34 \checkmark$$

$$18 = x - 4$$
$$18 + 4 = x - 4 + 4 \leftarrow \textbf{Add 4 to each side.}$$
$$22 = x \qquad \leftarrow \textbf{Simplify.}$$

Check: $\quad 18 = x - 4$
$$18 \overset{?}{=} 22 - 4$$
$$18 = 18 \checkmark$$

Show your steps to solve each equation. Then check.

1. $\qquad n + 5 = 11$

$$n + 5 - \square = 11 - \square$$
$$n = \square$$

Check: $\quad n + 5 = 11$
$$\square + 5 \overset{?}{=} 11$$
$$\square = 11$$

2. $\qquad 13 + b = 27$

$$13 + b - \square = 27 - \square$$
$$b = \square$$

Check: $\quad 13 + b = 27$
$$13 + \square \overset{?}{=} 27$$
$$\square = 27$$

3. $y - 18 = 24$

_____

_____

Check: _____

_____

_____

4. $15 = x - 8$

_____

_____

Check: _____

_____

_____

5. $5.7 + y = 19.4$

_____

_____

Check: _____

_____

_____

6. $2.3 + n = 4.5$

_____

_____

Check: _____

_____

_____

Solve each equation.

7. $a + 9 = -8$

$a = $ _____

8. $42 = d + 12$

$d = $ _____

9. $e + 3.7 = -7.8$

$e = $ _____

10. $6 = f + 12$

$f = $ _____

11. $-18 = s + (-23)$

$s = $ _____

12. $w + 4 = \frac{1}{2}$

$w = $ _____

Reteaching

Reteaching 3-3 Solving Equations by Dividing or Multiplying

To solve equations by division or multiplication:

① Use opposite, or inverse, operations to isolate the variable.

② Simplify.

③ Check by substituting your answer for the variable.

Solve and check each equation.

$8t = 56$

$\dfrac{8t}{8} = \dfrac{56}{8}$ ← **Divide each side by 8.**

$t = 7$ ← **Simplify.**

Check: $8t = 56$

       $8 \cdot 7 \overset{?}{=} 56$

         $56 = 56$ ✓

$\dfrac{w}{5} = 20$

$5 \cdot \dfrac{w}{5} = 5 \cdot 20$ ← **Multiply each side by 5.**

$w = 100$ ← **Simplify.**

Check: $\dfrac{w}{5} = 20$

       $\dfrac{100}{5} \overset{?}{=} 20$

         $20 = 20$ ✓

Show your steps to solve each equation. Then check.

1. $3x = 18$

$\dfrac{3x}{\square} = \dfrac{18}{\square}$

$x = 6$

Check: $3x = 18$

$3 \cdot \boxed{} \overset{?}{=} 18$

$\boxed{} = 18$

2. $\dfrac{y}{-5} = -13$

$\dfrac{y}{-5} \cdot \boxed{} = -13 \cdot \boxed{}$

$y = \boxed{}$

Check: $\dfrac{y}{-5} = -13$

$\dfrac{\boxed{}}{-5} \overset{?}{=} -13$

$\boxed{} = -13$

3. $y \cdot 8 = 24$

_____

_____

Check: $y \cdot 8 = 24$

_____

_____

_____

Solve each equation.

4. $-16 = -8x$

$x = $ _____

5. $\dfrac{b}{0.4} = 1.6$

$b = $ _____

6. $7.5 = 1.5c$

$c = $ _____

7. $-3r = 24$

$r = $ _____

8. $5d = 85$

$d = $ _____

9. $30t = -390$

$t = $ _____

10. $4h = 0$

$h = $ _____

11. $20j = 4{,}000$

$j = $ _____

12. $2.5 = -1.25w$

$w = $ _____

Reteaching 3-4 Solving Two-Step Equations

Michael bought 4 books for the same price at a fair. Admission to the fair was $5. How much was each book if Michael spent a total of $17 at the fair?

Follow these steps to solve the two-step equation: $4b + 5 = 17$

① Add or subtract on each side.

$$4b + 5 - 5 = 17 - 5$$
$$4b = 12$$

② Multiply or divide to isolate the variable.

$$\frac{4b}{4} = \frac{12}{4}$$
$$b = 3 \quad \leftarrow \textbf{Each book cost \$3.}$$

③ Check by substituting your answer for the variable.

Check: $4b + 5 = 17$
$$4 \cdot 3 + 5 \stackrel{?}{=} 17$$
$$17 = 17 \checkmark$$

___

Show your steps to solve each equation. Then check.

1. $2k + 5 = 25$

$$2k + 5 - \square = 25 - \square$$
$$\frac{2k}{\square} = \frac{20}{\square}$$
$$k = \square$$

Check: $2k + 5 = 25$
$$2 \cdot \square + 5 \stackrel{?}{=} 25$$
$$\square = 25$$

2. $\frac{p}{2} - 2 = 2$

$$\frac{p}{2} - 2 + \square = 2 + \square$$
$$\frac{p}{2} \cdot \square = 4 \cdot \square$$
$$p = \square$$

Check: $\frac{p}{2} - 2 = 2$
$$\frac{\square}{2} - 2 \stackrel{?}{=} 2$$
$$\square = 2$$

3. $7y - 17 = -38$

_____

_____

_____

Check: _____

_____

_____

Solve each equation.

4. $\frac{x}{-2} + 6 = 4$

$x =$ _____

5. $14j - 7 = 91$

$j =$ _____

6. $240a - 3 = 5$

$a =$ _____

7. $2.4 = 3s - 0.6$

$s =$ _____

8. $2 + \frac{n}{-5} = 4$

$n =$ _____

9. $140 = -4 - 12e$

$e =$ _____

Reteaching 3-5 Problem-Solving Strategy: Write an Equation

You can write equations to solve many types of problems.

Read   Caroline made 20 muffins. She put them into 3 boxes. She had 2 muffins left. How many muffins are in each box if each box has the same number of muffins?

Plan   Equation with words: $\dfrac{\text{total}}{\text{muffins}} = \left(\begin{array}{c} 3 \cdot \text{number of muffins} \\ \text{in each box} \end{array} \right) + 2 \text{ extra}$

Translate: Let m = number of muffins in each box.

Equation with symbols: $20 = 3m + 2$

Solve
$$20 - 2 = 3m + 2 - 2$$
$$18 = 3m$$
$$\frac{18}{3} = \frac{3m}{3}$$
$$6 = m$$

There are 6 muffins in each box.

Look Back   Check your answer.
6 muffins in each of 3 boxes plus 2 extra = 20 muffins.

Write an equation to solve each problem. Check the solution.

1. Harold bought 2 pairs of sandals for the same price. He also bought a pair of socks for $3. How much did one pair of sandals cost if Harold spent a total of $31?

   _____

   _____

   _____

2. Jessica added 120 to one third a number for a result of 200. What is the number?

   _____

   _____

   _____

3. Kim, Kyle, and Kate contribute the same amount to their father's gift. Their older sister contributes $12. How much does Kate contribute if the total for the gift is $30?

   _____

   _____

   _____

4. David has 4 boxes of apples. Each box has the same number of apples. After David eats 3 apples, there are 109 apples left in the boxes. How many apples were in each box?

   _____

   _____

   _____

▪▪▪▪ Reteaching 3-6 Simplifying and Solving Equations

Combining terms can help solve equations.

Solve: $5n + 6 + 3n = 22$

$$\begin{aligned} 5n + 3n + 6 &= 22 \quad \leftarrow \textbf{Commutative} \\ 8n + 6 &= 22 \qquad\quad \textbf{property} \\ 8n + 6 - 6 &= 22 - 6 \\ 8n &= 16 \\ \frac{8n}{8} &= \frac{16}{8} \\ n &= 2 \end{aligned}$$

Check: $5n + 6 + 3n = 22$
$$5(2) + 6 + 3(2) \overset{?}{=} 22$$
$$22 = 22 \ ✔$$

When an equation has a variable on both sides, add or subtract to get the variable on one side.

Solve: $-6m + 45 = 3m$
$$\begin{aligned} -6m + 6m + 45 &= 3m + 6m \quad \leftarrow \textbf{Add 6m} \\ 45 &= 9m \qquad\qquad \textbf{to each} \\ \frac{45}{9} &= \frac{9m}{9} \qquad\qquad \textbf{side.} \\ 5 &= m \end{aligned}$$

Check: $-6m + 45 = 3m$
$$-6(5) + 45 \overset{?}{=} 3(5)$$
$$15 = 15 \ ✔$$

Solve each equation.

1. $a - 4a = 36$

$a =$ _____

2. $3b - 5 - 2b = 5$

$b =$ _____

3. $5n + 4 - 8n = -5$

$n =$ _____

4. $12k + 6 = 10$

$k =$ _____

5. $3(x - 4) = 15$

$x =$ _____

6. $y - 8 + 2y = 10$

$y =$ _____

7. $3(s - 10) = 36$

$s =$ _____

8. $-15 = p + 4p$

$p =$ _____

9. $2g + 3g + 5 = 0$

$g =$ _____

10. $6c + 4 - c = 24$

$c =$ _____

11. $3(x - 2) = 15$

$x =$ _____

12. $4y + 9 - 7y = -6$

$y =$ _____

13. $4(z - 2) + z = -13$

$z =$ _____

14. $24 = -2(b - 3) + 8$

$b =$ _____

15. $17 = 3(g + 3) - g$

$g =$ _____

16. $5(k - 4) + 3k = 4$

$k =$ _____

17. $8 - m - 3m = 16$

$m =$ _____

18. $6n + n + 14 = 0$

$n =$ _____

19. $7(p + 1) + p = 9$

$p =$ _____

20. $36 = 4(q - 5)$

$q =$ _____

21. $25 = 5(t + 2) - 2t$

$t =$ _____

Reteaching

Reteaching 3-7 Formulas

You can use a **formula** to find the area of a figure.

Find the area of a square with side length 1.2 m.

$A = s \cdot s$ ← **Write the formula.**
$A = (1.2)(1.2)$ ← **Substitute known values.**
$A = 1.44$ ← **Simplify.**

The area of the square is 1.44 m².

Area Formulas
Rectangle: A = length · width $A = lw$
Square A = side length · side length $A = s \cdot s$
Trapezoid: $A = \frac{1}{2}$ height (sum of bases) $A = \frac{1}{2}h(b_1 + b_2)$

Knowing how to transform a formula by solving for one of its variables can be useful.

Write a formula to find the width of a rectangle.

Use $A = lw$. Solve for w.

$$\frac{A}{l} = \frac{lw}{l}$$

$$\frac{A}{l} = w, \text{ or } w = \frac{A}{l} \quad ← \textbf{The desired formula.}$$

Find the area of each figure.

1. Square: side 3.4 ft

2. Rectangle: 6 m × 2.3 m

3. Trapezoid: $b_1 = 6$ m, $b_2 = 12$ m, $h = 4.2$ m

_____

Solve each formula for the variable indicated.

4. Solve for r.
$d = rt$

5. Solve for l.
$A = lw$

6. Solve for b.
$y = rx + b$

_____

7. Solve for t.
$I = prt$

8. Solve for h.
$A = bh$

9. Solve for h.
$V = lwh$

_____

Reteaching 3-8 Inequalities

An **inequality** compares one expression with another.
A **solution** of an inequality is any value of the variable that makes
the inequality true.

5 is a solution of the inequality $x \geq -1$ because $5 \geq -1$.

You can graph inequality solutions on a number line.

Inequality	Graph	How to Read the Graph
$x > 2$ x is *greater than* 2		An open dot at 2 shows that 2 is not included. All numbers greater than 2 are included.
$x < 2$ x is *less than* 2		An open dot at 2 shows that 2 is not included. All numbers less than 2 are included.
$x \geq 2$ x is *equal to or greater than* 2		A solid dot at 2 shows that 2 is included. All numbers greater than 2 are also included.
$x \leq 2$ x is *equal to or less than* 2		A solid dot at 2 shows that 2 is included. All numbers less than 2 are also included.

State whether each number is a solution of $x \leq 3$.

1. 0 _____   **2.** -4 _____   **3.** 4 _____   **4.** 1 _____

Graph each inequality on a number line.

5. $x > -2$

6. $y \leq -1$

7. $4 \geq a$

8. $t \geq 0$

9. $k < -3$

Reteaching

Reteaching 3-9 *Solving Inequalities by Subtracting or Adding*

To help solve an inequality, you can subtract the same number
from or add the same number to each side.

Solve $x + 5 > 8$.

$$x + 5 > 8$$
$$x + 5 - 5 > 8 - 5 \quad \leftarrow \textbf{Subtract 5}$$
$$\textbf{from each side.}$$
$$x > 3 \quad \leftarrow \textbf{Simplify.}$$

Graph the solution.

$$\xleftarrow{\quad\quad} \underset{-2\ -1\ \ 0\ \ 1\ \ 2\ \ 3\ \ 4}{+\!\!+\!\!+\!\!+\!\!+\!\!\oplus\!\!+} \xrightarrow{\quad}$$

Solve $y - 4 \leq 1$.

$$y - 4 \leq 1$$
$$y - 4 + 4 \leq 1 + 4 \quad \leftarrow \textbf{Add 4}$$
$$\textbf{to each side.}$$
$$y \leq 5 \quad \leftarrow \textbf{Simplify.}$$

Graph the solution.

$$\xleftarrow{\quad} \underset{-1\ \ 0\ \ 1\ \ 2\ \ 3\ \ 4\ \ 5}{+\!\!+\!\!+\!\!+\!\!+\!\!+\!\!\bullet} \xrightarrow{\quad}$$

Solve each inequality. Graph the solution.

1. $9 + a > 11$ _____

2. $-4 + r < 0$ _____

3. $2 > n - 1$ _____

4. $1 + s \leq 5$ _____

5. $m + 2 \geq -1$ _____

6. $-3 + q < -5$ _____

7. $4 < x + 1$ _____

8. $y + 2 \geq 1$ _____

Reteaching 3-10 Solving Inequalities by Dividing or Multiplying

To help solve an inequality, you can divide or multiply each side by the same number. However, if the number is a negative number, you must also reverse the direction of the inequality.

Solve $-3y \geq 6$. Graph the solution.

$$-3y \geq 6$$

$$\frac{-3y}{-3} \leq \frac{6}{-3} \quad \leftarrow \textbf{Divide each side by } -3.$$
$$\textbf{Reverse the direction}$$
$$\textbf{of the inequality.}$$

$$y \leq -2 \quad \leftarrow \textbf{Simplify.}$$

Graph:

$$\leftarrow\!\!\!-\!\!+\!\!+\!\!\bullet\!\!+\!\!+\!\!+\!\!+\!\!\rightarrow$$
$$-4\ -3\ -2\ -1\ \ 0\ \ 1\ \ 2$$

Solve $\frac{a}{2} > 1$. Graph the solution.

$$\frac{a}{2} > 1$$

$$2\frac{a}{2} > 1(2) \quad \leftarrow \textbf{Multiply each side by 2.}$$

$$a > 2 \quad \leftarrow \textbf{Simplify.}$$

Graph:

$$\leftarrow\!\!\!+\!\!+\!\!+\!\!+\!\!\oplus\!\!+\!\!+\!\!\rightarrow$$
$$-2\ -1\ \ 0\ \ 1\ \ 2\ \ 3\ \ 4$$

Solve each inequality. Graph the solution.

1. $2a > 8$ _____

$$\leftarrow\!\!+\!\!+\!\!+\!\!+\!\!+\!\!+\!\!+\!\!+\!\!+\!\!+\!\!+\!\!\rightarrow$$
$$-5\ -4\ -3\ -2\ -1\ \ 0\ \ 1\ \ 2\ \ 3\ \ 4\ \ 5$$

2. $12 < -3r$ _____

$$\leftarrow\!\!+\!\!+\!\!+\!\!+\!\!+\!\!+\!\!+\!\!+\!\!+\!\!+\!\!+\!\!\rightarrow$$
$$-5\ -4\ -3\ -2\ -1\ \ 0\ \ 1\ \ 2\ \ 3\ \ 4\ \ 5$$

3. $\frac{1}{3}n > 1$ _____

$$\leftarrow\!\!+\!\!+\!\!+\!\!+\!\!+\!\!+\!\!+\!\!+\!\!+\!\!+\!\!+\!\!\rightarrow$$
$$-5\ -4\ -3\ -2\ -1\ \ 0\ \ 1\ \ 2\ \ 3\ \ 4\ \ 5$$

4. $12 \geq 6s$ _____

$$\leftarrow\!\!+\!\!+\!\!+\!\!+\!\!+\!\!+\!\!+\!\!+\!\!+\!\!+\!\!+\!\!\rightarrow$$
$$-5\ -4\ -3\ -2\ -1\ \ 0\ \ 1\ \ 2\ \ 3\ \ 4\ \ 5$$

5. $\frac{m}{4} < 1$ _____

$$\leftarrow\!\!+\!\!+\!\!+\!\!+\!\!+\!\!+\!\!+\!\!+\!\!+\!\!+\!\!+\!\!\rightarrow$$
$$-5\ -4\ -3\ -2\ -1\ \ 0\ \ 1\ \ 2\ \ 3\ \ 4\ \ 5$$

6. $5q \geq 5$ _____

$$\leftarrow\!\!+\!\!+\!\!+\!\!+\!\!+\!\!+\!\!+\!\!+\!\!+\!\!+\!\!+\!\!\rightarrow$$
$$-5\ -4\ -3\ -2\ -1\ \ 0\ \ 1\ \ 2\ \ 3\ \ 4\ \ 5$$

7. $-4x \leq 8$ _____

$$\leftarrow\!\!+\!\!+\!\!+\!\!+\!\!+\!\!+\!\!+\!\!+\!\!+\!\!+\!\!+\!\!\rightarrow$$
$$-5\ -4\ -3\ -2\ -1\ \ 0\ \ 1\ \ 2\ \ 3\ \ 4\ \ 5$$

Reteaching

Enrichment: Minds on Math

For Lessons 3-1 through 3-3

3-1

How many numbers from 0 to 1,000 have digits that have a sum of 10?

3-2

On a recent airline flight there was 1 empty seat for every 3 passengers. If there were 132 seats available, how many passengers were on the flight?

3-3

Look for a pattern in the equations below. Then find the value of 75^2, 85^2, and 95^2.

$15^2 =\ \ \ 225$
$25^2 =\ \ \ 625$
$35^2 = 1,225$
$45^2 = 2,025$
$55^2 = 3,025$
$65^2 = 4,225$

■■■ Enrichment: Minds on Math   *For Lessons 3-4 through 3-6*

3-4

Les, Quinn, Shari, and Nate shared a box of pencils equally. Quinn then shared all of the pencils he got equally with 5 other friends. If Quinn and each of his friends got 3 pencils, how many pencils were in the box?

3-5

Which positive one-digit numbers do * and # stand for in the expressions below?

$$\frac{* + \#}{* - \#} = 1\frac{1}{2} \qquad \frac{* + 4 \cdot \#}{* - 4 \cdot \#} = 9$$

3-6

Derrick is thinking of a negative integer. When he multiplies the integer by itself and then adds three times the integer to the product, he gets 180. What is Derrick's integer?

Enrichment: Minds on Math   *For Lessons 3-7 through 3-10*

3-7

Tim has more than 50 marbles but less than 100 marbles. He gets a remainder of 6 when he divides the number of marbles by either 8 or 9. How many marbles does Tim have?

3-8

Write the numbers 1 through 7 in the circles so that the numbers in each line of connected circles total 12.

3-9

Look for a pattern in the equations below. Then find the value of $199^2 - 198^2$ and $2{,}150^2 - 2{,}149^2$.

$1^2 - 0^2 = 1$
$2^2 - 1^2 = 3$
$3^2 - 2^2 = 5$
$4^2 - 3^2 = 7$
$5^2 - 4^2 = 9$

3-10

Change the operation in one place in the expression below to make the value 100.

$1 + 2 + 3 + 4 + 5 + 6 + 7 + 8 + 9$

Backpack Take-Home Activities *For use with Chapter 3*

Dear Family,

These activities provide an opportunity for you and your child to share knowledge of mathematics. I invite you to choose one or two activities and complete them together. Please have your child return the family project(s) to me by _____.

Materials: merchandise catalog • yardstick • stopwatch or watch with a second hand • nine books • paper • pencil

SHOPPING BY CATALOG

Have family members take turns browsing through a catalog, finding an item that he or she would like to purchase, and writing down the name and price of the item. If each family member has saved $10.00, does the person have enough money to purchase the chosen item? Work with family members to write variable expressions to show how much more money each person needs. (A *variable expression* is an equation in which a symbol, usually a letter, is used to represent a number or range of numbers. Example: $2 + n = 8$) Finally, discuss ways family members might earn money to purchase their chosen items.

STEP BY STEP

Go outside and use a yardstick to measure a distance of 50 yards. Have each family member predict how long it will take him or her to walk 50 yards. Write down each prediction. Then have each family member walk the 50 yards. Use a watch or stopwatch to time his or her walk. Study the results. Work with family members to write equations that show the difference between each person's estimated time and the actual time.

STACK IT UP!

Use nine books to make two stacks of books. For example, one stack might have four books; the other stack would have five books. Make a table that indicates the different ways the books can be stacked. Write equations that describe the different ways to make the stacks. Example: $4 + 5 = 9$.

WHAT DO YOU THINK?

Please take a few moments to let me know how you enjoyed these activities. Write your comments on the back of this sheet and have your child return it to me by _____.

▬▬▬**Checkpoint 1**

Simplify each expression.

1. $3(6 - x)$

2. $3y + 2(y - 6)$

3. $6t - 7 - 7t$

_____   _____   _____

Solve each equation. Check the solution.

4. $15 = -3w$

5. $z - 31 = 98$

6. $3m - 5 = 13$

_____   _____   _____

7. Danielle bought music scores for $4 each and a pair of drumsticks for $6. The total cost was $26. Write and solve an equation to find the number of music scores Danielle bought.

_____

- -

▬▬▬**Checkpoint 2**

Solve each equation. Check the solution.

1. $-15 = 3(c - 2)$

2. $7b = 3b + 28$

3. $-13 = 4n - 7 - n$

_____   _____   _____

Solve each inequality. Graph the solution on a number line.

4. $x + 6 > 4$

5. $w - 7 \geq -13$

6. $16 < x + 13$

_____   _____   _____

7. Circle A, B, C, or D. Which equation would you use to solve this problem? Carl bought a baseball hat on sale for $8.75. This was $2.50 less than the original price of the hat. What was the original price of the hat?

A. $x + 2.50 = 8.75$

B. $x - 2.50 = 8.75$

C. $8.75 = 2.50 - x$

D. $x + 8.75 = 2.50$

8. A bus traveled 270 mi at 45 mph. Use the formula $d = rt$ to find how many hours the bus traveled.

_____

Chapter 3 Student Self-Assessment Survey

1. Now that you have finished this chapter, think about what you have learned about algebra. Check each topic that you feel confident you understand.

_____ simplify expressions and combine like terms (3-1)

_____ solve equations by subtracting or adding (3-2)

_____ solve equations by dividing or multiplying (3-3)

_____ solve two-step equations (3-4)

_____ write and solve equations to solve problems (3-5)

_____ use the distributive property to solve equations (3-6)

_____ solve equations with variables on both sides of the equal sign (3-6)

_____ use formulas to solve problems (3-7)

_____ solve formulas for another value (3-7)

_____ write and graph inequalities (3-8)

_____ solve inequalities by subtracting or adding (3-9)

_____ solve inequalities by dividing or multiplying (3-10)

2. Before the Chapter Assessment, I need to review _____

_____

3. **a.** Check one. In general, I thought this chapter was
____ a snap ____ easy ____ average ____ hard ____ a monster
b. Why do you feel this way?

_____

4. In this chapter, I did my best work on _____

_____

5. In this chapter, I had trouble with _____

6. This chapter is about algebra. Based on this chapter, do you think you will like doing more work in algebra? Explain.

_____

7. Did you use a computer spreadsheet in this chapter? _____
What are some situations in which people use spreadsheets outside the classroom?

_____

Assessment

Chapter 3 Performance Assessment

Time to Talk

Anthony wants his own telephone. His parents said he can have one if he pays for it himself. Use this chart to help Anthony decide whether he can afford his own phone from the Talk-A-Lot Telephone Company.

TALK-A-LOT TELEPHONE COMPANY CHARGES	
Installation:	$42
Deposit:	$50
Basic Monthly Charge:	$8

Show all of your work on a separate sheet of paper.

1. To earn money, Anthony mows lawns for $4 an hour. First, he wanted to find the least number of hours needed to pay for the installation and deposit. He wrote this inequality:

    $$4H \geq 42 + 50$$

    Describe what each term in this inequality represents. Then solve for H.

2. Next Anthony wanted to find the least number of hours he would have to work to pay his basic monthly charge. He wrote this inequality:

    $$4H \geq 8$$

    Describe what each term in this inequality represents and solve the inequality for H.

3. Anthony has two out-of-state friends whom he would like to call. He discovered the following about long-distance calls:

    *   The phone company charges one price for the first minute and then a lower price per minute for every minute thereafter.

    *   If a customer talks for any part of a minute, he or she is charged for the whole minute.

    *   Rates vary according to the time of day.

    Anthony looked up the rates to the two cities where his

Chapter 3 Performance Assessment (continued)

friends live. He used this information to make the following price chart. (*N* represents the number of minutes after the first minute.)

TELEPHONE CALL RATES IN CENTS			
City Called	Day Rate	Evening Rate	Night/Weekend Rate
Youngstown	$27 + 23N$	$21 + 17N$	$16 + 12N$
Central City	$22 + 18N$	$18 + 15N$	$12 + 8N$

Compare the rates for the times of day and between the two cities. Explain each relationship.

4. Complete the chart below to show the cost of a 5-minute call to each city at each of the different times.

COSTS FOR A 5-MINUTE CALL			
City Called	Day	Evening	Night/Weekend
Youngstown			
Central City			

5. Anthony didn't want his long-distance calls to total more than $9.88. He decided he would call his friends only on weekends and talk the same number of minutes to each friend.

   a. Write and solve an inequality that could be used to find the number of minutes he could talk to each friend.

   b. Using your answer above, explain in words how long he could talk to each friend.

Excursion

Pretend you have a telephone and that two of your good friends live in Youngstown and Central City. Use the Talk-A-Lot Telephone Company charges to describe how much it will cost you for a full year of telephone service. Include the initial charges and describe the long-distance calls you might make to Youngstown or Central City. Explain how you could pay your phone charges.

Chapter 3 Performance Assessment Scoring Rubric

Exercise	Points	Explanation
1.	2	H = number of hours he needs to work; 42 = installation; 50 = deposit; $4H$ = total amount he would earn for working H hours; $H \geq 23$ h
	1	Incorrect explanation but correct value for H
	0	Incorrect explanation AND incorrect value for H
2.	1	H = number of hours he needs to work; $4H$ = total amount he would earn for working H hours; 8 = basic monthly charge; $H \geq 2$ h
	0	No explanation of B OR incorrect value
3.	2	Daytime is most expensive, night/weekend is cheapest; calls to Youngstown are more expensive; good explanations
	1	Half of above information, including explanation
	0	Less than half of above information
4.	2	Youngstown: $1.19, $.89, $.64; Central City: $.94, $.78, $.44
	1	Four or five correct amounts
	0	Fewer than four correct amounts
5. a.	2	Equivalent to $988 \geq 16 + 12N + 12 + 8N; N \leq 48$ min
	1	Incorrect setup of inequality OR incorrect reading of chart
	0	Incorrect setup of inequality AND incorrect reading of chart
b.	1	He could speak to each friend for up to 48 minutes
	0	Incorrect response
Excursion	5	Amount without long-distance charges is $92 + 12(\$8) = \$188$; good explanation
	4	Amount without long-distance charges is $188; one amount omitted from total; good explanation
	3	One or more computational errors; partial explanation
	2	Process error, but no computational errors; partial explanation
	1	Process AND computational errors; partial or no explanation
	0	No response

Chapter 3 Assessment • Form A

Answers

1. Simplify $-10x - 3(x - 2)$.

1. _____

2. Simplify $6(y - 1) + 3(-2y + 2)$.

2. _____

3. Solve $p + 49 = -10$.

3. _____

4. Derrick spent $17.95 on dinner and a movie. He has $4.35 left. Write and solve an equation to find the amount of money that Derrick had originally.

4. _____
_____

5. Solve $\frac{x}{5} = 17$.

5. _____

6. A stereo costs $306. Shirley saves $9 per week to buy the stereo. Write and solve an equation to find how many weeks Shirley must save.

6. _____
_____

7. Solve $4y + 7 = -9$.

7. _____

8. For an end of the year bonus, each person in the company received $50. In addition, the shipping department received an extra bonus of $500 to be shared equally. Each worker in the shipping department received a total of $75. Write and solve an equation to find how many workers are in the shipping department.

8. _____
_____

9. Solve $-5n + 6 = 5n - 4$.

9. _____

10. Solve $-8 + 6(y - 2) = -38$.

10. _____

11. Find the perimeter and area of a square with a side of 7 cm.

11. _____
_____

12. Find the average speed of an airplane that travels 2,880 mi in 6 h.

12. _____

13. Solve $A = \frac{1}{2} bh$ for h.

13. _____

14. Solve $81 > -9w$.

14. _____

Assessment

Chapter 3 Assessment • Form A (continued)

15. Write an inequality for the graph below.

$$\begin{array}{ccccccccc} -4 & -3 & -2 & -1 & 0 & 1 & 2 & 3 & 4 \end{array}$$

16. Solve $y - 2 < -7$. Graph the solution.

15. _____

16. _____

17. Allan has \$30.00. He wants to order some pizzas which sell for \$7.99. He also wants to give a \$2.00 tip. Write an inequality that shows how many pizzas Allan can order.

17. _____

18. If you add 176 to half a number, the result is 199. Write and solve an equation to find the number.

18. _____

19. Solve $p + 7 \leq -11$.

19. _____

Circle A, B, C, or D.

20. Solve $\frac{m}{3} > -9$.

   A. $m > -3$ **B.** $m > -27$

   C. $m > 3$ **D.** not here

20. _____

Choose a Strategy

21. Ali wants to buy a show horse that costs \$1,500. She plans to put \$800 down and pay the rest in 5 equal payments. What will be the amount of each payment? Write and solve an equation.

21. _____

Writing

22. The formula $A = \frac{1}{2}h(b_1 + b_2)$ is used to find the area of a trapezoid. Explain how to change the formula to find the height.

_____

_____

Chapter 3 Assessment • Form B

Choose the best answer. Circle A, B, C, or D.

1. Simplify $5x - 2(x - 4)$.
   A. $3x - 4$ B. $3x + 8$ C. $7x + 4$ D. $7x + 8$

2. Simplify $7(y + 3) - 4(3y + 6)$.
   A. $-5y + 3$ B. $-5y - 3$ C. $19y + 3$ D. $-19y - 45$

3. Solve $q - 68 = -43$.
   A. 111   B. -111 C. 25   D. -25

4. Marguerite spent \$21.98 on dinner and bowling. She has \$8.75 left. Which equation could you use to find the amount of money Marguerite had originally?
   A. $m - 21.98 = 8.75$ B. $m - 8.75 = -21.98$
   C. $m = 21.98 - 8.75$ D. $m + 21.98 = 8.75$

5. Solve $\frac{y}{12} = 48$.
   A. 36   B. 4   C. 576   D. 6

6. Kevin wants to buy a CD player that costs at least \$499. He saves \$15 each week to buy the CD player. Which inequality could you use to find the number of weeks Kevin must save?
   A. $15w \geq 499$ B. $w + 499 \leq 15$
   C. $15(499) \geq w$ D. $\frac{w}{499} \geq 15$

7. Solve $9p + 7 = -11$.
   A. $-\frac{4}{9}$ B. 2   C. -2 D. $-\frac{9}{4}$

8. The picnic committee decided that the charge for this year's fund-raiser picnic is \$10 per family plus \$2 for each person in the family. Which equation could you use to find the number of people in a family if the family paid \$36?
   A. $2p = 36 + 10$ B. $10 - 2p = 36$
   C. $36 - 10 = -2p$ D. $2p + 10 = 36$

9. Solve $-8r - 4 = 7r - 4$.
   A. -8 B. -1 C. 0   D. 8

10. Solve $7 - 3(y - 2) = 19$.
    A. $\frac{-32}{3}$ B. $\frac{-14}{3}$ C. -2 D. not here

Assessment

Chapter 3 Assessment • Form B *(continued)*

11. The width of a rectangle is 6 cm shorter than its length. The perimeter is 28 cm. Find the length and width.

    A. $l = 4$ cm, $w = 10$ cm   **B.** $l = 24$ cm, $w = 4$ cm

    C. $l = 10$ cm, $w = 4$ cm   **D.** $l = 5.5$ cm, $w = 8.5$ cm

12. Two less than three times a number is equal to 16. What is the number?

    A. $\frac{14}{3}$ **B.** 8   **C.** 6   **D.** 0

13. An airplane traveled 3,965 mi from Berlin to New York in 7 h. What was the plane's speed rounded to the nearest ten?

    A. 60 mi/h   **B.** 570 mi/h   **C.** 5,660 mi/h   **D.** not here

14. The circumference formula for a circle is $C = 2\pi r$. Solve the formula for r.

    A. $r = \frac{C}{2\pi}$ **B.** $r = \frac{2\pi}{C}$ **C.** $r = 2\pi C$ **D.** $r = C - 2\pi$

15. Solve $3y \geq -21$.

    A. $y \geq -7$ **B.** $y \geq 7$ **C.** $y \leq 7$ **D.** $y \leq -7$

16. Solve $t - 3 < -17$.

    A. $t < -14$ **B.** $t < -20$ **C.** $t > -14$ **D.** $t < 20$

17. Solve $\frac{a}{-5} \leq 20$.

    A. $a \leq -4$ **B.** $a \leq -100$ **C.** $a \geq -100$ **D.** $a \geq -4$

18. Solve $-3y = -171$.

    A. -174 **B.** -57 **C.** 57   **D.** 513

19. Which inequality matches the graph below?

    A. $x > 6$ **B.** $x \geq 6$ **C.** $x \leq -6$ **D.** $x \leq 6$

20. Solve $m + 8 \geq -5$.

    A. $m > -5$ **B.** $m \geq 3$ **C.** $m \geq -13$ **D.** $m \leq 13$

Choose a Strategy

21. Antonio wants to buy a car that costs $2,500. He plans to put $400 down and pay the rest in six equal payments. Find the amount of each payment.

    A. $400   **B.** $350   **C.** $375   **D.** $300

Chapter 3 Cumulative Review

Choose the best answer. Circle A, B, C, or D.

1. There are 4 red socks, 6 green socks, and 8 blue socks in a drawer. You choose one sock at random. What is the probability of choosing a red sock?

   A. $\frac{1}{18}$ **B.** $\frac{1}{4}$

   C. $\frac{2}{9}$ **D.** $\frac{2}{5}$

2. What is the mode of this data?
   18, 81, 79, 58, 81, 49

   A. 61   **B.** 63

   C. 68.5   **D.** 81

3. The median of three numbers is 23. The range is 20. The mean is 21. What are the three numbers?

   A. 21, 23, 41   **B.** 20, 21, 23

   C. 10, 23, 30   **D.** Not here

4. Graph $x > 3$.

   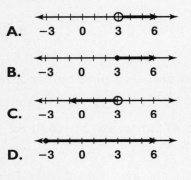

   A. -3 0 3 6

   B. -3 0 3 6

   C. -3 0 3 6

   D. -3 0 3 6

5. Simplify 3^{-3}.

   A. -9 **B.** 0

   C. $\frac{1}{27}$ **D.** $\frac{1}{9}$

6. Which expression has the same value as $x^2 - 6x + 2$ for $x = 5$?

   A. $2x - x^6 + 2$ **B.** $6x - 33$

   C. $2x + 7$ **D.** $-x^2 + 6x - 2$

7. Anna's mother is 4 years older than 3 times Anna's age. If Anna is y years old, which expression describes her mother's age?

   A. $3y - 4$ **B.** $3y + 4$

   C. $4y + 3$ **D.** $37y$

8. Write 3.59×10^{-4} in standard form.

   A. 0.000359   **B.** 0.0359

   C. 3,590   **D.** 35,900

9. Twelve more than twice a number is -8. What is the number?

   A. -16 **B.** -10

   C. 2   **D.** not here

10. Adam keeps track of the hours he spends playing hockey, baseball, and soccer. Which kind of graph should he draw to show the time playing hockey compared to the total time for all three sports?

    A. bar graph   **B.** line graph

    C. scatter plot   **D.** circle graph

11. Solve $14c + 9 = 13c - 9$.

    A. -18 **B.** 18

    C. 9   **D.** 0

12. Use mental math to find $(-7) + 3 + (-6) + 10$.

    A. 0   **B.** 10

    C. -13 **D.** -26

Chapter 3 Cumulative Review (continued)

13. Compare $-25x$ ▇ $25x$ for $x = -2$.

    A. $>$ **B.** $<$

    C. $=$ **D.** $\leq$

14. Find $-54 \div (-1) \div (-4 - 2)$.

    A. 54   **B.** -27

    C. -9 **D.** 3

15. Which of the following is *not* true about the integers 10 and -10?

    A. Their sum is zero.

    B. They are additive inverses.

    C. They are opposites.

    D. Their difference is zero.

16. Which expression could you use to show a deposit of $38, a withdrawal of $4, and another withdrawal of $13?

    A. $38 - ($4 + $13)$

    B. $4 + $13 - 38

    C. $38 - $4 + 13

    D. $13 - $4 + 38

17. Evaluate $5a^2 - 10a$ for $a = -2$.

    A. 40   **B.** 10

    C. 0   **D.** -10

18. Which of the following properties is demonstrated by this equation?
    $7(x + y) = 7x + 7y$

    A. the addition property of equality

    B. the multiplication property of equality

    C. the distributive property

    D. the identity property

19. Solve $6y - 12 = 0$.

    A. 0   **B.** 6

    C. 12   **D.** 2

20. Mark and two friends mowed lawns this summer and made $1,125. At the end of the summer, they divided their total earnings equally. Mark had enough money to buy a bicycle and deposit $250 in the bank. Which equation can help you find the amount Mark paid for his new bicycle?

    A. $x + 250 = 1,125$

    B. $3(x + 250) = 1,125$

    C. $x = \frac{1125}{3} + 250$

    D. $x(3 + 250) = 1,125$

21. Solve $-5x > 20$.

    A. $x > 15$ **B.** $x < 100$

    C. $x > -100$ **D.** $x < -4$

22. Find $-6 + 3(-5)$.

    A. -21 **B.** 9

    C. 15   **D.** not here

23. Evaluate $-9m + 7$ for $m = -2$.

    A. -11 **B.** 0

    C. 25   **D.** not here

Use the stem-and-leaf plot below for Exercises 24–25.

Number of Concerts Performed

1	0 1 3 4
2	1 2 5 6
3	0 2 2 4 7

$2 \mid 1$ means 21

24. What is the range?

    A. 13   **B.** 27

    C. 37   **D.** 47

25. What is the median?

    A. 10   **B.** 23.6

    C. 25   **D.** 32

1. $2x + 3$ **2.** $3x + 1$ **3.** $x - 6$ **4.** $11b$

5. $5z$ **6.** $-4b$ **7.** $-3t$ **8.** $2m$

9. $-3j$ **10.** $-10v$ **11.** $-h$ **12.** $-9x$

13. $3k$ **14.** $-3s$ **15.** q **16.** $7n$

17. $-9j$ **18.** $-5j$ **19.** $8x$ **20.** $5; 12; 60$

21. $z; 6; z; 3; 18$ **22.** $12d - 72$ **23.** $9m + 63$

24. $4a + 2$ **25.** $2x + 4y$ **26.** $5x + 1$

27. $5q + 5$ **28.** $9n - 3$ **29.** $5r - 1$

30. $5a - 17$ **31.** $3x - 2y$ **32.** $2n$

33. $-2b + c + 5$ **34.** $-6z - 2$ **35.** $-3b + 32$

36. $x + y - 9$ **37.** 6

38. Answers may vary. Sample: A term is a part of a variable expression separated by plus or minus signs. You can combine terms if they have the same variable. For example, $x + 3x - 7 + y = 4x + y - 7$.

39. Answers may vary. Samples— three terms: $m + 2m + 8$; four terms: $m + 2m + 3 + 5$.

40a. Subtract 9, then divide by 10.

b. $10n + 15; 10n + 9$

c. The simplified form of the steps is $10n + 9$. To undo it, use the opposite operations, subtraction and division.

41a.

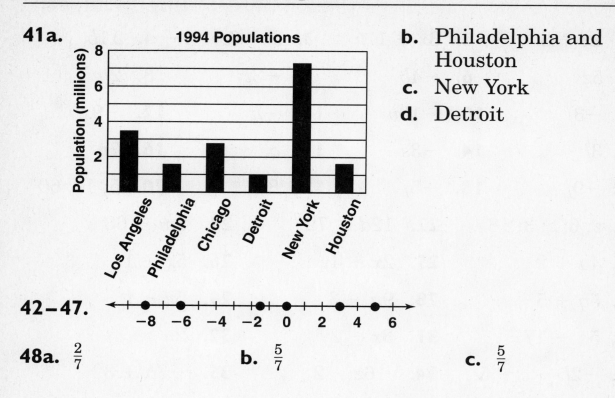

b. Philadelphia and Houston

c. New York

d. Detroit

42–47.

48a. $\frac{2}{7}$ **b.** $\frac{5}{7}$ **c.** $\frac{5}{7}$

1. $x + 1 = 4$; 3

2. $x - 2 = -6$; -4

3. $x + 2 = -4$; -6

4. -24

5. 30

6. -7.7

7. -2

8. -3

9. $7\frac{1}{2}$

10. -6

11. -422

12. $-5\frac{1}{2}$

13. -1.2

14. -4

15. 28

16. $7\frac{2}{3}$

17. 1,355

18. -46

19. -4.3

20. D

21. 5

22. 6

23. 27

24. -9

25. 21

26. 0

27. -14

28. -18

29. $18,700 = a - 13,900$; \$32,600

30. $x + 8 = 52$; 44 invitations

31. $34 - 16 = x$; 18 tooth extractions

32. $t = 12 - 15$; $-3°F$

33. -7

34. -21

35. 9.09

36. 12.5

37. $4\frac{1}{2}$

38. -20

39. 20.75

40. 127

41. -10.07

42. $11\frac{1}{2}$

43. -20

44. -4.25

45. Sample: Over the past two days Kristin earned \$11.55. Today she earned \$8.40. How much did she earn yesterday? [\$3.15]

46. 3

47. $-3, 3$

48. no solution

49. 0

50. $-1, 1$

51. $-3, 1$

52. -20

53. 57

54. 3

55. 17

56. -11

57. -5

58a. You get the equation $0 = 0$. **b.** all real numbers
  c. Answers may vary. Sample: $2x + 3 = x + 1 + x + 2$

59.

Data	Tally	Frequency
22	II	2
23	II	2
24	I	1
25	III	3
26	II	2
27	II	2

60.

61. -3 **62.** -10 **63.** -14 **64.** -4

65. 431×52; check students' work for reasoning.

1. $2x = -10; -5$ **2.** $9 = 3x; 3$ **3.** $4x = 12; 3$

4. 7   **5.** -5 **6.** -19 **7.** -4 **8.** -40

9. 6   **10.** $-\frac{1}{2}$ **11.** -12 **12.** 4   **13.** 50

14. -11 **15.** -23 **16.** 0   **17.** $\frac{1}{3}$ **18.** -0.25

19a. $9x = 180; \$20$ **b.** $12y = 180; 15$ wk

20. 20   **21.** -24 **22.** -80.8 **23.** -8 **24.** 256

25. -40 **26.** 450   **27.** 7   **28.** -0.7 **29.** -6

30. 150   **31.** -18 **32.** 0   **33.** -20 **34.** -160

35. $8p = 9.84; \$1.23$ **36.** $m = 2 \cdot 1{,}500; 3{,}000$ calls

37. $a = 8 \cdot 8; 64\%$ **38.** no; $25(-5) \neq -5$

39. yes; $\frac{15}{(-5)} = -3$ **40.** no; $-15 \neq \frac{(-5)}{-3}$

41. yes; $10 = -2(-5)$ **42.** yes; $-5(-5) = 25$

43. Answers may vary. Sample: Four streets form a square city block 0.8 mi on each side. How long is the curb around the entire block? [$P = 4(0.8); 3.2$ mi]

Answers for Mixed Review, p. 130

44.

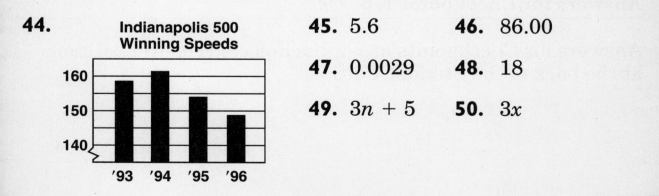

Indianapolis 500 Winning Speeds

45. 5.6   **46.** 86.00

47. 0.0029   **48.** 18

49. $3n + 5$ **50.** $3x$

1. 4   2. 25   3. -8 4. 0

5. 40   6. -7 7. 3   8. $-\frac{4}{9}$

9. -324 10. 6   11. 31   12. 16

13. -1 14. -4 15. -30 16. -36

17. 1   18. 1,560   19. 0   20. $-2,100$

21. 44   22. 4   23. 5   24. -54

25. C

26. You must add 9 to each side of $3v - 9 = 12$ before dividing by 3, and you only have to divide by 3 to solve $3v = 12$.

27. $7   28. 81 g   29. 309 orders   30. $570

31. Check students' work; 14.

Answers for Mixed Review, p. 134

32. 5   33. $\frac{1}{3}$ 34. $\frac{1}{81}$ 35. $\frac{1}{36}$

36. 1   37. 30   38. 18   39. 20

40. 24   41. 66   42. 20,602 ft

Answers for Checkpoint 1, p. 134

Answers for Checkpoints are in the Selected Answers section at the back of the Student Edition.

1. $(7 - 2)x = 35$; 7 mi
2. $8x + 45 = 325$; $35
3. $4x - 4 = 60$; 16 V/m
4. $\frac{x}{2} + 236 = 950$; 1,428
5. 64, 65
6. 24 gal
7. $78
8. music: $725; refreshments: $675; decorations: $250; supplies $45
9. 22 h
10. 20 in., 28 in.

Answers for Mixed Review, p. 137

11. Answers may vary. Sample: What are your 5 favorite TV programs?
12. Answers may vary. Sample: Which do you prefer to watch, fun cartoons or boring news?
13. 0.0035
14. 0.078
15. 0.359
16. 0.0008
17. 0.1426
18. 0.00632
19. 15 and -27, 27 and -15

Answers for Lesson 3-6 *On Your Own* Exercises, pp. 140–141

1. 2   **2.** 1   **3.** −2   **4.** 10

5. 9   **6.** 5   **7.** 2   **8.** −2

9. 7   **10.** −1   **11.** 5   **12.** 10

13. $\frac{-2}{5}$ **14.** 5   **15.** −5   **16.** 3

17. 33   **18.** Check students' work.

19. 46 g   **20.** 8   **21.** −1   **22.** 3

23. −3   **24.** −18   **25.** 3.2   **26.** 2

27. 5   **28.** −10   **29.** 9   **30.** 7

31. 4   **32.** 4   **33.** $4m + 5 = 21; 4$

34. $3y + 505 = 1{,}000; 165$

Answers for Mixed Review, p. 141

35. Check students' work.   **36.** 9   **37.** 216

38. 625   **39.** 1   **40.** 64   **41.** −64

42. 7 children

1. 36 cm

2. 22.8 m

3. 18 ft

4. 38.44 cm^2

5. 20 m^2

6. 136 ft^2

7. 15 in.^{2}

8. 24 m^2

9. 0.25 cm^2

10. 14 in.

11. 12 m

12. 712.5 mi

13. You must isolate the variable to solve; the solution may contain another variable.

14a. 48 mi/h

b. 9:18 P.M.

15. $n = 4(F - 37)$, or $n = 4F - 148$

16. $b = \frac{A}{h}$

17. $t = \frac{d}{r}$

18. $r = \frac{C}{2\pi}$

19. $d_2 = \frac{2A}{d_1}$

20. $p = \frac{I}{rt}$

21. $\ell = \frac{P - 2w}{2}$

22. $w = \frac{V}{\ell h}$

23. $b = y - mx$

24. $m = \frac{y - b}{x}$

25a. $h = \frac{2A}{b_1 + b_2}$

b. 9.5 ft

26a. $C = \frac{5}{9}(F - 32)$

b. 20°C

c. Fahrenheit boiling point is 212° and freezing point is 32°. Fahrenheit scale measures temperature in the U.S. Celsius boiling point is 100° and freezing point is 0°. Celsius scale measures temperature outside the U.S. Kelvin boiling point is 373.15° and freezing point is 273.15°. Kelvin scale is used by laboratory scientists.

Answers for Mixed Review, p. 145

27. 2,030,000

28. 0.0000429

29. 0.00324

30. 5,350,000

31. 0.0798

32.

8	3
9	0 4 7 8
10	0 5
11	2
12	5 7
13	4 9

33. 102.5

34. 56

35. 25 of each coin

8 | 3 represents 83

1. no; $-4 < -1$ **2.** yes; $6 > -1$ **3.** yes; $0 > -1$

4. no; $-6\frac{1}{2} < -1$ **5.** no; $-1 = -1$ **6.** yes; $3.2 > -1$

7. $k \le 0$ **8.** $w \ge 6.75$

9. $p \le 40$ **10.** $d \ge 12$

11. s = number of stops; $s > 85$ **12.** s = speed; $s \le 35$

13. h = height in in.; $h \ge 50$ **14.** b = bread loaves; $b < 8$

15. s = number of students; $s \le 400$

16. m = money for museum; $m \ge 85$

17. s = number of students; $s \le 65$

18. c = number of chairs; $c \ge 30$

19. $x > -1$ **20.** $x \le 0$

21. $x \ge -2$ **22.** $x < 1$

23.

25.

27.

29.

31.

33.

24.

26.

28.

30.

32.

34.

35. $<$ **36.** $>$ **37.** B

38. Each solution can be graphed on a number line; an equation has only one solution while an inequality has many.

39. Check students' work.

40. $h \le 65\%$

41. $t \ge 90°$

42a.

      b. $t > -4$ **c.** yes; $-3.5 > -4$

  d. The graph would include -4; $t \ge -4$.

43a. s = number of schools; $s > 95,000$.
  b. d = dollars spent; $d > 200,000,000,000$.
  c. u = number of colleges and universities; $u \le 4,000$.
  d. n = number of part-time U.S. college students;
    $n \le 7,000,000$.

Answers for Mixed Review, p. 151

44. mean: 30.25; median: 34.5

45. mean: 72.25; median: 75.5

46. $<$ **47.** $<$ **48.** $<$ **49.** $=$ **50.** $.85

Answers

1. 2   **2.** 4   **3.** 8   **4.** 1.2

5a. $x < -2$

  b. Answers may vary. Sample: For $x = -5$, $(-5) + 7 < 5$ is true because $2 < 5$. For $x = 0$, $(0) + 7 < 5$ is false because $7 > 5$.

  c. $(-2) + 7 < 5$ is false, so -2 is not a solution.

  d. Solve the inequality and substitute numbers from each side of the solution number as well as the number itself.

  e. Check students' work.

6. $m < -6$

7. $s \geq -19$

8. $x \geq 6$

9. $y > 1{,}300$

10. $d < 4$ **11.** $m < 2\frac{1}{2}$

12. $x \geq -6$ **13.** $n \geq -3$

14. $n > -1.5$ **15.** $y \geq -24$

16. $k < 2\frac{1}{4}$ **17.** $b > -7{,}200$

18. $t + 17 > 65$; $t > 48$; it was above 48°F.

19. $9 + 8 + 10 + 9 + x \geq 45$; $x \geq 9$; Amy must score at least 9 points.

20. $n > 11$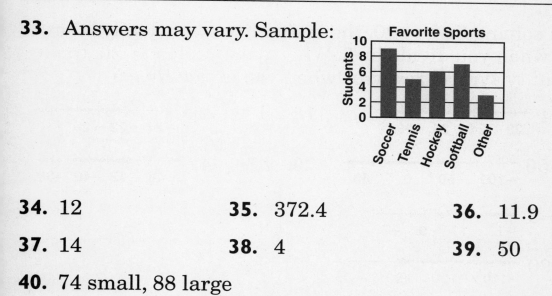
   9 11 13 15

21. $x \geq -1$
  −3 −1 1 3

22. $f \geq -11$
  −13 −11 −9 −7

23. $b > 43$
  41 43 45 47

24. $x \geq -88$
  −88   0

25. $r < 0$
  −4 −2 0 2

26. $w \leq 1$
  −2 0 2

27. $w \geq 11.9$
  11.8 11.9 12.0 12.1

28. $z < -2\frac{1}{2}$
  −4 −3 −2 −1

29. $n \leq -948$
  −948 0

30. $x \leq 4$
  0 2 4 6

31. $b \leq 2.1$
  1.8 2.0 2.2

32. You must deposit a minimum of $31.37.

Answers for Mixed Review, p. 156

33. Answers may vary. Sample:

Favorite Sports

Soccer, Tennis, Hockey, Softball, Other (Students)

34. 12   **35.** 372.4   **36.** 11.9

37. 14   **38.** 4   **39.** 50

40. 74 small, 88 large

Answers for Checkpoint 2, p. 156

Answers for Checkpoints are in the Selected Answers section at the back of the Student Edition.

1. $p > 7$

2. $x \geq -4$

3. $b > 4$

4. $x \geq 7$

5. $c < -2$

6. $q < -5$

7. $t \leq -5$

8. $m < 8$

9. $y \leq 8$

10. $j < 3$

11. $x \geq -14$

12. $z > 2$

13. $x < -6.2$

14. $c \geq 6$

15. $x < 2$

16. When solving $5x > -20$, the inequality symbol stays the same when you divide by 5. When solving $-5x > 20$, the inequality symbol reverses when you divide by -5.

17. $d > 24$

18. $n \geq -22$

19. $r > -50$

20. $b \geq -42$

21. $m < -9$

22. $j \leq -90$

23. $y < 3,200$

24. $k < -5$

25. $y > 0$

26. $d < -96$

27. $t > -2$

$$\overset{\xleftarrow{\hspace{1em}}\overset{\oplus}{\underset{-4\quad -2\quad 0\quad 2}{\hspace{2em}}}\xrightarrow{\hspace{1em}}}{}$$

28. $x \geq -6$

$$\overset{\xleftarrow{\hspace{1em}}\overset{\bullet}{\underset{-8\quad -6\quad -4\quad -2}{\hspace{2em}}}\xrightarrow{\hspace{1em}}}{}$$

29. $n < -12$

$$\overset{\xleftarrow{\hspace{1em}}\overset{\oplus}{\underset{-16\ -14\ -12\ -10}{\hspace{2em}}}\xrightarrow{\hspace{1em}}}{}$$

30. $x \geq -36$

$$\overset{\xleftarrow{\hspace{1em}}\overset{\bullet}{\underset{-42\ -36\ -30\ -24}{\hspace{2em}}}\xrightarrow{\hspace{1em}}}{}$$

31. $n > 25$

$$\overset{\xleftarrow{\hspace{1em}}\overset{\oplus}{\underset{20\quad 25\quad 30\quad 35}{\hspace{2em}}}\xrightarrow{\hspace{1em}}}{}$$

32. $x < 6$ **33.** $n \geq 2$ **34.** $m < 6$ **35.** $b \leq 20$

36. $\frac{x}{-3} \leq 15$; $x \geq -45$; the number is at least -45.

37. $3x \geq 150$; $x \geq 50$; each earned at least \$50.

38. $\frac{175}{x} \geq 15$; $x \leq 12$; Hector will pay his loan in 12 mo or less.

39. 7 tapes

Answers for Mixed Review, p. 160

40. -7 **41.** 1   **42.** -48

43. -20 **44.** 9   **45.** 35, 42, 49

46. 12, 10, 8   **47.** 45, 55, 65   **48.** 48, 96, 192

49. 45

Answers for Wrap Ups are in the Selected Answers section at the back of the Student Edition.

Answers for Chapter 3 Assessment, p. 164

1a. $4r + 2$ **b.** $-4t + 5$ **c.** $6m - 4$ **d.** $-28f - 8g - 5$

2. The equation $x + 2 = 1$ and the inequality $x + 2 < 1$ can both be solved by subtracting 2 from each side. The equation $-3x = 15$ and the inequality $-3x < 15$ can both be solved by dividing each side by -3; however, since you are dividing by a negative number, the direction of the inequality must be reversed.

3. Answers may vary. Sample: Kelly needs \$4 to see a movie. She owes her sister \$12. How much should she earn each day to pay for both in 3 days? ($\$5\frac{1}{3}$)

4a. 9 **b.** -1 **c.** -85 **d.** 10

5. D **6a.** $3x + 5 = x + 7; 1$ **b.** \$.23

7. 2.5 h **8a.** 169 cm^2 **b.** 4 in.^2 **c.** 13.5 m^2

9a. $s = \frac{P}{4}$ **b.** $d = \frac{C}{p}$ **c.** $b = \frac{2A}{h}$

10a. d = driver's age; $d \geq 16$
 b. p = number of passengers; $p \leq 5$
 c. w = number of weeks; $w < 3$
 d. t = number of tickets; $t \leq 75$

11. $-3x \geq 15; x \leq -5$
$\begin{array}{ccccc} & -9 & -7 & -5 & -3 \end{array}$
12. A

13a. $w < 15$
$\begin{array}{cccc} 11 & 13 & 15 & 17 \end{array}$
 b. $y > 5$
$\begin{array}{cccc} 3 & 5 & 7 & 9 \end{array}$

 c. $z \leq 15$
$\begin{array}{cccc} 11 & 13 & 15 & 17 \end{array}$
 d. $s \leq -16$
$\begin{array}{cccc} -20 & -18 & -16 & -14 \end{array}$

Answers for Chapter 3 Cumulative Review, p. 165

1. C **2.** C **3.** A **4.** D **5.** B **6.** D
7. B **8.** B **9.** C **10.** E **11.** C

Chapter 3 Support File Answers

Technology Activity 3-2

Exercises
1. 94   **2.** −57   **3.** 1.83   **4.** $-\frac{1}{4}$ **5.** −20, 20
6. −10, 10   **7.** −30, −10   **8.** $n + 15 = 38$;
23 newsletters   **9.** $m - 5.65 = 9.35$; $15

The Problem
$c - 6.75 = 56.50$; $63.25

Math Connection Activity 3-10

Exercises
1a.
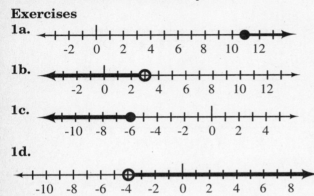

1b.

1c.

1d.

The Problem
$\frac{1}{6}x \geq 4$, $x \geq 24$

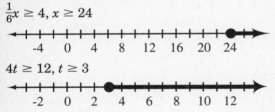

$4t \geq 12$, $t \geq 3$

Practice 3-1

1. $6a + 7$ **2.** $8k - 72$ **3.** $9n$ **4.** $7w + 21$
5. $5b - 21$ **6.** $12 + 8t$ **7.** $14 + 3k$ **8.** $3j$
9. $6d - 48$ **10.** $8x + 39$ **11.** $4m + 21$
12. $2f - 11$ **13.** $12v - 8$ **14.** $9g + 47$
15. $9h - 1$ **16.** $5e - 44$ **17.** $4y + 7$
18. $2.13m + 1.8$ **19.** $64k + 252$
20. $3.09j + 14.214$ **21.** $36b - 1{,}008$
22. $5.86y + 8.4$ **23.** $4.3c + 24.08$ **24.** $98x - 255$
25. $5.2c + 10.9d$ **26.** $63m - 11$
27. $8j + 4k + 20$ **28.** $5.29r + 14.42s$
29. $72c - 2d + 43$ **30.** $9a + 8b - 2$
31. $15.3g + 2q + 3.79$ **32.** Let n be the
number. $(2n + 6) \div 2 = n + 3$, $(n + 3) = n$. You
get the number you started with.

Practice 3-2

1. −12   **2.** −22   **3.** 15.53   **4.** $\frac{17}{24}$ **5.** 18
6. −31   **7.** 28.59   **8.** 6   **9.** 45   **10.** 17   **11.** 13.3
12. $\frac{7}{8}$ **13.** −19   **14.** 6.03   **15.** 33   **16.** −5
17. −23   **18.** 16.5   **19.** 0.42   **20.** −39   **21.** 41
22. −23   **23.** $\frac{3}{20}$ **24.** −20   **25.** $n + 7 = 25$;
18 boxes   **26.** $K - 27.98 = 18.76$; $46.74
27. $t - 4 = 28$; 32 books   **28.** $m + 8 = 20$;
12 dozen

Practice 3-3

1. −12   **2.** −32.4   **3.** 20   **4.** 19   **5.** 0   **6.** 17
7. −2.4   **8.** 61.42   **9.** −4.7   **10.** 963   **11.** −21
12. −6.3488   **13.** −72   **14.** 77.744   **15.** −7.5
16. −65.86   **17.** 2.06   **18.** −475   **19.** −79
20. −39.984   **21.** −24.6   **22.** 8,091   **23.** 2.9
24. −4,935   **25.** −119   **26.** −5   **27.** 69.92
28. −9   **29.** $12n = 15.48$; $1.29   **30.** $\frac{c}{7} = 12.95$;
$90.65   **31.** $12f = 96$; 8 dozen   **32.** $\frac{b}{5} = 157.90$;
$789.50

Practice 3-4

1. 2   **2.** 2   **3.** −12   **4.** 90   **5.** 1   **6.** −77
7. −8.7   **8.** −0.8   **9.** 5.2   **10.** −91.7228   **11.** 14
12. 190   **13.** 1   **14.** 21.47   **15.** 7   **16.** 780
17. −6   **18.** −52.93   **19.** $100 + 20w = 460$;
18 wk   **20.** $50 + 2v = 144$; 47 visits

1. 2	4	■	2. 5	1
5	■	■	7	■
■	■	3. 7	■	■
4. 5	4	2	5. 9	■
4	■	■	6. 2	8

Practice 3-5

1. $9.20 = .56 + .32(x - 1)$; 28 min
2. $2(104) + 2x = 576$; 184 ft   **3.** $\frac{4}{5}t = 12.6$;
15.75 gal   **4.** $\frac{1}{3}n - 9.4 = 8.7$; 54.3
5. $t(t - 1) = 812$; 28 and 29   **6.** $210
7. 3 hours

Practice 3-6

1. $2x + 5 = 3x + 3$; $x = 2$ **2.** $2x + 4 = x + 9$; $x = 5$ **3.** 1 **4.** 4 **5.** -21 **6.** 2.4 **7.** -2 **8.** -2.5 **9.** 4 **10.** -96 **11.** -8.25 **12.** -7 **13.** 11 **14.** 2 **15.** -7.5 **16.** 32 **17.** 3 **18.** 5 **19.** -9.5 **20.** -6 **21.** 2 **22.** 3.75

Practice 3-7

1. $P = 2l + 2w$; $A = l \cdot w$; $P = 33.2$ cm; $A = 67.2$ cm^2 **2.** $P = a + b + c$; $A = \frac{1}{2}b \cdot h$; $P = 47$ cm; $A = 80$ cm^2 **3.** $P = 2a + 2b$; $A = bh$; $P = 62$ in.; $A = 168$ in.^{2} **4.** $P = a + b + c + d$; $A = \frac{1}{2}h\,(b_1 + b_2)$; $P = 90$ m; $A = 442$ m^2 **5.** $8s = 400$; 50 mi/h **6.** $4.5 \times 515 = d$; 2,317.5 mi **7.** $12t = 18$; 1.5 h **8.** 32°F **9.** 212°F **10.** -20°C **11.** 25°C

Practice 3-8

1. $x \le 1$ **2.** $x > 4$ **3.** $x \ge -3$ **4.** $x > 0$ **5.** $x \ge -2$ **6.** $x \le -4$ **7.** $x \ge 1$ **8.** $x < 2$ **9.** $x > 3$ **10.** $x \le 0$

11.

12.

13.

14.

15.

16.

17.

18.

Practice 3-9

1. $m > -4$

2. $q \le 5$

3. $w > -3$

4. $y < -1$

5. $k \le 3$

6. $u \ge 2$

7. $x < -3$

8. $d \ge 1$

9. $h < -3$

10. $e \ge 10$

11. $g \le 5$

12. $r > -5$

13. $x + 8 < 24$; less than 16 in.
14. $235 + n > 462$; more than 227 points

Practice 3-10

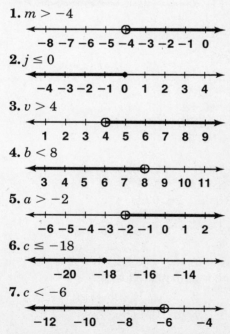

1. $m > -4$

2. $j \le 0$

3. $v > 4$

4. $b < 8$

5. $a > -2$

6. $c \le -18$

7. $c < -6$

8. $i \geq 4$

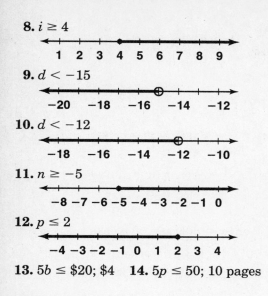

9. $d < -15$

10. $d < -12$

11. $n \geq -5$

12. $p \leq 2$

13. $5b \leq \$20; \$4$ **14.** $5p \leq 50$; 10 pages

Reteaching 3-1

1. $8x$ **2.** $3c$ **3.** $-2h$ **4.** y **5.** $-4m$ **6.** $7n$
7. $-4s$ **8.** $-3t$ **9.** $-6b$ **10.** $-7p$ **11.** $10v$
12. $-3j$ **13.** $8c - 40$ **14.** $4d + 24$ **15.** $6n + 3$
16. $2x + 3y$ **17.** $-2m + 4$ **18.** $5v - 20$
19. $-4a + 3$ **20.** $5s - 1$ **21.** $-2u + 12$
22. $6x + y - 9$ **23.** $-2x - 3y$ **24.** $5v$
25. $-3s + 2$ **26.** $3x + 8$ **27.** $j - 2k$ **28.** $3a - 5$

Reteaching 3-2

1. 5; 5; 6; 6; 11   **2.** 13; 13; 14; 14; 27
3. $y - 18 + 18 = 24 + 18$; $y = 42$; $y - 18 = 24$;
$42 - 18 \stackrel{?}{=} 24$; $24 = 24$ **4.** $15 + 8 \stackrel{?}{=} x - 8 + 8$;
$23 = x$; $15 = x - 8$; $15 \stackrel{?}{=} 23 - 8$; $15 = 15$
5. $5.7 + y - 5.7 = 19.4 - 5.7$; $y = 13.7$;
$5.7 + y = 19.4$; $5.7 + 13.7 \stackrel{?}{=} 19.4$; $19.4 = 19.4$
6. $2.3 + n - 2.3 = 4.5 - 2.3$; $n = 2.2$;
$2.3 + n = 4.5$; $2.3 + 2.2 \stackrel{?}{=} 4.5$; $4.5 = 4.5$ **7.** -17
8. 30   **9.** -11.5 **10.** -6 **11.** 5   **12.** $-3\frac{1}{2}$

Reteaching 3-3

1. 3; 3; 6; 18   **2.** -5; -5; 65; 65; -13
3. $\frac{y \cdot 8}{8} = \frac{24}{8}$; $y = 3$; $3 \cdot 8 \stackrel{?}{=} 24$; $24 = 24$ **4.** 2
5. 0.64   **6.** 5   **7.** -8 **8.** 17   **9.** -13 **10.** 0
11. 200   **12.** -2

Reteaching 3-4

1. 5; 5; 2; 2; 10; 10; 25   **2.** 2; 2; 2; 2; 8; 8; 2
3. $7y - 17 + 17 = -38 + 17$; $\frac{7y}{7} = \frac{-21}{7}$; $y = -3$;
$7y - 17 = -38$; $7 \cdot -3 - 17 \stackrel{?}{=} -38$; $-38 = -38$
4. 4   **5.** 7   **6.** $\frac{1}{30}$ **7.** 1.0   **8.** -10 **9.** -12

Reteaching 3-5

1. $2x + 3 = 31$; $s = 14$; One pair cost \$14.
2. $120 + \frac{n}{3} = 200$; $n = 240$; The number is 240.
3. $3k + 12 = 30$; $k = \$6$; Kate contributes \$6.
4. $4a - 3 = 109$; $a = 28$; There were 28 apples
in each box.

Reteaching 3-6

1. -12 **2.** 10   **3.** 3   **4.** $\frac{1}{3}$ **5.** 9   **6.** 6   **7.** 22
8. -3 **9.** -1 **10.** 4   **11.** 7   **12.** 5   **13.** -1
14. -5 **15.** 4   **16.** 3   **17.** -2 **18.** -2 **19.** $\frac{1}{4}$
20. 14   **21.** 5

Reteaching 3-7

1. $A = 11.56 \text{ ft}^2$ **2.** $A = 13.8 \text{ m}^2$ **3.** $A = 37.8 \text{ m}^2$
4. $r = \frac{d}{t}$ **5.** $l = \frac{A}{w}$ **6.** $b = y - rx$ **7.** $t = 1\frac{I}{pr}$
8. $h = \frac{A}{b}$ **9.** $h = \frac{V}{lw}$

Reteaching 3-8

1. yes   **2.** yes   **3.** no   **4.** yes
5.
6.
7.
8.
9.

Reteaching 3-9

1. $a > 2$

2. $r < 4$

3. $n < 3$

4. $s \leq 4$

5. $m \geq -3$

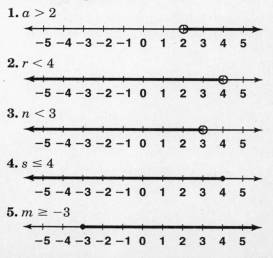

6. $q < -2$

<-----●----->
−5 −4 −3 −2 −1 0 1 2 3 4 5

7. $x > 3$

<-----●----->
−5 −4 −3 −2 −1 0 1 2 3 4 5

8. $y \geq -1$

<-----●----->
−5 −4 −3 −2 −1 0 1 2 3 4 5

Reteaching 3-10

1. $a > 4$

<-----●----->
−5 −4 −3 −2 −1 0 1 2 3 4 5

2. $r < -4$

<-----●----->
−5 −4 −3 −2 −1 0 1 2 3 4 5

3. $n > 3$

<-----●----->
−5 −4 −3 −2 −1 0 1 2 3 4 5

4. $s \leq 2$

<-----●----->
−5 −4 −3 −2 −1 0 1 2 3 4 5

5. $m < 4$

<-----●----->
−5 −4 −3 −2 −1 0 1 2 3 4 5

6. $q \geq 1$

<-----●----->
−5 −4 −3 −2 −1 0 1 2 3 4 5

7. $x \geq -2$

<-----●----->
−5 −4 −3 −2 −1 0 1 2 3 4 5

Enrichment/Minds on Math

3-1 63 numbers   **3-2** 99 passengers
3-3 $75^2 = 5,625$; $85^2 = 7,225$; $95^2 = 9,025$
3-4 72 pencils   **3-5** * = 5; # = 1   **3-6** −15
3-7 78 marbles   **3-8** Sample answer is shown.

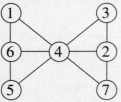

3-9 397; 4,299
3-10 $1 + 2 + 3 + 4 + 5 + 6 + 7 + 8 \times 9 = 100$

Checkpoint I

1. $18 - 3x$ **2.** $5y - 12$ **3.** $-t - 7$ **4.** -5
5. 129   **6.** 6   **7.** $4n + 6 = 26$; $n = 5$

Checkpoint 2

1. -3 **2.** 7   **3.** -2 **4.** $x > -2$ **5.** $w \geq -6$
6. $3 < x$ **7.** B   **8.** 6 h

Chapter 3 Assessment Form A

1. $-13x + 6$ **2.** 0   **3.** -59
4. $m - 17.95 = 4.35$; $m = \$22.30$ **5.** 85
6. $\frac{306}{x} = 9$ or $9x = 306$; $x = 34$ weeks   **7.** -4
8. $\frac{500}{x} + 50 = 75$; $x = 20$ workers   **9.** 1   **10.** -3
11. $P = 28$ cm; $A = 49$ cm^2 **12.** 480 mi/h
13. $h = \frac{2A}{b}$ **14.** $-9 < w$ **15.** $x \geq -3$
16. $y < -5$

<-----●----->
−6 −5 −4 −3 −2 −1 0

17. $2 + 7.99x \leq 30$ **18.** $176 + \frac{1}{2}x = 199$; $x = 46$
19. $p \leq -18$ **20.** B   **21.** $1,500 = 800 + 5x$;
$140   **22.** Multiply both sides of the equation
by 2. Then divide both sides by $(b_1 + b_2)$.

Chapter 3 Assessment Form B

1. B   **2.** B   **3.** C   **4.** A   **5.** C   **6.** A   **7.** C   **8.** D
9. C   **10.** C   **11.** C   **12.** C   **13.** B   **14.** A
15. A   **16.** A   **17.** C   **18.** C   **19.** D   **20.** C
21. B

Chapter 3 Cumulative Review

1. C   **2.** D   **3.** C   **4.** A   **5.** C   **6.** B   **7.** B
8. A   **9.** B   **10.** D   **11.** A   **12.** A   **13.** A   **14.** C
15. D   **16.** A   **17.** A   **18.** C   **19.** D   **20.** B
21. D   **22.** A   **23.** C   **24.** B   **25.** C